1

Cover Photo - Bulkley River, Telkwa, British Columbia, Canada
Taken in 2014 by Diana Pritchard

LETTER TO MY CHILDREN

Dear Martin, Ella, and Inga,

I thought I would start writing a letter to you all as a way of recording my history. You have asked me many times to keep a diary and make notes but as is often the case, I start and never manage to continue. You might find, however, quite a lot of information in reading my poems. Many of them are, of course, written to record events or just to expand various thoughts and themes but within them you might find things about my character and way of thinking. Anyway, I hope this letter will put things in perspective for you so that you get to know me better.

Mum

"If you have the words, there's always a chance that you'll find the way." - *Seamus Heaney*

for John,
my ever-patient husband

Published by ShortCliff
ISBN 978-1-9196144-0-3

CHAPTERS

PHOTOS

PROLOGUE

"Freeedah! Get the aaaxe," my younger brother called out.

He was in the depths of a dream, and he wanted to scream but found his voice was muffled. Something was causing him to choke. The others heard him call out and shook him awake. He was inside the stomach of a bear and he needed to get out. What better way to do so than to get his little sister to wield an axe, kill the bear and pull him out. How had the bear caught him in the first place and why was he dreaming about bears anyway? We all had our dreams and when we found ourselves overwhelmed with fear from the reports of wild animals, particularly grizzly bears, black bears, cougars or even wolves in the vicinity, we all dealt with that fear in different ways.

We had an assortment of axes lying about the place as there was plenty of firewood needing to be chopped and my brothers were often set to the task. Not without accident, I might add. The axe Paul had wanted Freda to use may well have been the one that found his knee one day and which sent him to hospital to have twenty odd stitches put in. I wonder sometimes how we all survived the back country living we all had, mostly seeing that we were very much 'off grid.'

My brother Jon, just fourteen months younger than me, had done much the same thing a couple of years before Paul chopped his knee. The axe he was swinging while he held a piece of wood on the chopping block so he could make kindling, found his thumb. That was an accident to remember. His thumb was just hanging in a bit of skin, and I remember the blood and mother binding his hand with thumb in place before he was off to the hospital sixteen miles away. Poor boy, he had to have an operation to join the severed tendon and then spent many months squeezing a ball with his hand in order to strengthen the muscles. We all thought it was amazing how the thumb was attached back in place and the story of how he had to have his arm opened up so they could join the tendon with what we were told was 'cat gut,' fascinated us.

Then, of course, there was me. I managed to step on a six-inch nail that was poking through a length of shiplap that had been left lying on the ground. It pushed its way so far in that I could see a little red dot on the top of my foot. Luckily, it didn't break the surface, but it meant I had to hobble about for most of one summer. I also twisted my foot and ankle badly in an accident at the sawmill. The worst thing that happened though was while doing some training with my running spikes on, sprinting circuits of the field next to my mother's garden. She asked me if I would stop and help by lifting one end of the gate up which wasn't yet fixed properly to the fence. As I did so, I stepped backwards, and I could feel my spikes crunch into her bones. I had the whole weight of the heavy timber joists, as well as my own weight, focused on her foot. You can imagine how awful I felt. My mother screamed, of course, there was blood everywhere and I just wanted to run away. In fact, I think I may have done so. Luckily, my brothers were there to help bind a T-shirt around it and she managed to struggle the half mile up the hill to the house. Their memory of the incident was of seeing their mother with her foot in a bowl of water that had turned bright red. They looked on wide eyed seeing what 'their big sister did' to their mum.

We remember these things. Accidents were all around us. At school we would hear about the drowning of a classmate in the raging river, or the girl called Elizabeth who was in my brother's class and fell through the ice by the Telkwa River Bridge. Children were all helping on the farms and in the bush. One boy lost his arm to a power saw accident and another boy called Billy, who was a neighbour or ours, lost his life by falling in front of a baler during harvest. Even the school playground posed a danger. It was located at the base of a hill which, in winter, was used for skiing and it was there that my brother broke his leg. Danger lurked in every corner and as we had a great amount of freedom, we had to learn the hard way sometimes.

The Northwest Interior of British Columbia just after the WW2 was a place where many felt they were mid-century pioneers. All were trying to make a living out of the land, forest and mines of the area. Most of the smallholders held two jobs. If they had a farm, they also worked in the bush part of the year and this was what our family did. We cleared land for raising cattle, grew crops and reaped the forest of timber to make lumber to sell. It was our way of life during my formative years.

As to dreams, I had mine. Not only bad ones created out of a fear of animals or human beings, but dreams about my future. When I was a teenager, I would often sit on a log and look up the valley towards the beautiful mountain and imagine someone, a handsome man perhaps, coming to whisk me away from the life I felt trapped in.

So it is that I consider myself as having had three lives. The first one was lived in Canada with my parents and took up my formative years. It was a life of paternal dominance and abuse that assured my silence. The second one changed me into an English girl but lead me into another type of controlled relationship ending in domestic violence with its repercussions. The third one I live now, settled in a lasting relationship, one son, two daughters, a grandchild and a voluntary position of twenty years giving help and advice to others less fortunate.

1 - HOW I CAME TO BE

This story about me started in the middle of the twentieth century at a time when the Second World War was still raging across the globe. Just as with all wars, people get disbursed from one area to another either by joining in the conflict and physically moving in order to take up arms, or, as civilians, having to move from the area of conflict. In my parents' case, it was my father, Filip Andreas Moen escaping from occupied Norway to join the war with the Norwegian Airforce based in Britain that brought my parents together. The story of my father's escape from Norway and his trek through Sweden and Finland to Murmansk in Russia is captured in a book written by his travelling companion Edvard Renan, called Wilderness to War. It follows their journey, often by raft, through a mosquito ridden arctic landscape eventually ending in a Russian prison camp where they managed to persuade their captors that they were not German escapees. Eventually they were released to sail with the famous arctic convoy to Britain where they were able to join the war effort. My father was based with the Norwegian Airforce in North Weald, Essex, but eventually joined the Norwegian Navy.

My mother, Elizabeth Jean Soper, was in the Women's Land Army on her own father's farm in Essex so the farm workers could join the war effort.

It was my mother's experience with farming that stood her in good stead when they eventually moved to Canada. Being the daughter of the farmer, she endeavoured to set an example to the other workers and put in far more hours than most. As she was a member of the Young Farmers' club, one of their dances was held at the village hall in North Weald and this is where my parents met. They eventually married just after the war had ended.

I was born on 27th September 1946 in a nursing home in Bell

Street, Sawbridgeworth, Hertfordshire, a village on the border with Essex and not far from Harlow. As I was my mother's first child, and as her own mother had died the previous month, it was considered better to give birth to me in a nursing home rather than at home. Home at that time was at New Hall Farm, in my grandfather's house. My brother Jon was born fourteen months later in the same house. The family doctor at the time was Dr. Booth who was also a family friend. He features later in my story.

Figure 1: Baby Me

There are photos of me playing in the garden and my earliest memory was of eating lettuce which the gardener, Mr. Wren, gave me when he was having his lunch break behind the house by the garden shed. One photo shows me wearing a flowery summer dress with smocking, riding on a small wooden tricycle with my blonde hair framing a rosy complexion. I was a little English toddler in a very English setting. The house was of a two-story Georgian style with grey bricks, a large lawn for tennis, two yew trees either side of the entrance and a walnut tree. There was also a kitchen garden with a tool shed potting sheds and a greenhouse behind. At the back there was a two roomed bungalow for the housekeeper which my grandfather had resorted to needing to employ since his wife had died. There were a lot of flowers and the whole front of the house was covered in Virginia creepers that turned bright red in the fall. It was a house I grew to know well later in my life but as I was a toddler, I remember little of it.

My grandfather had come to Harlow when my mother was about six years old. He started farming in Edmonton, North London by renting a few acres from the Eastern Railway Company where he grew potatoes. He ploughed his profits into this venture and was eventually able to obtain an agricultural mortgage on some land and to purchase the house in Old Harlow. His own father, who had a dairy and milk round in Chingford, Essex had moved with his father to Buntingford, Hertfordshire in 1886. The family had sold the farm called *Restinease* near Mevagissey, Cornwall and journeyed north by train with their eleven children, all their stock and a couple of employees with their families. They rented a farm from the Co-operative Society called *Little Hormead.*

My father worked at the farm after the war, where my grandfather had a herd of cattle, grew potatoes, and also raised award winning chickens. Perhaps my father had a view to getting involved in the running of the business while my mother dealt with the household and nursed their new baby. She must have missed her own mother, Dorothy, who had been a Red Cross nurse in the First World War. She would have been so helpful had she not died having long suffered from colon cancer. I know my mother missed her. As I grew older, she often told me about her dreams and how her mother featured in them.

However, after a holiday in Norway and because there seemed to be no long-term prospects for my father at New Hall, it was decided that they would explore the possibility of going to live in Canada. Although they had thought they might go to Norway to live, due to the war, there were not many jobs available, particularly in the northern area around North Trondelag and Steinkjer where the family lived. When they were first married, they tried living with my father's parents while he went to an agricultural college and my mother learned Norwegian, endeavouring to fit in with the lifestyle which was so different from her own. She tried hard to prove herself to the Norwegians but found it difficult. Norway at that time was experiencing much poverty and it was probably hard for them to accept my mother as they perceived her as being from a 'privileged' background. Eventually my father had a 'falling-out' with his own parents, so they returned to England.

During the time living at New Hall, when I was just learning to walk, I fell down the very steep stairs from top to bottom. Later, when I saw the stairs as an adult, I was quite shocked as to how steep they were. I was told that I cried but my father, who could not stand crying, gave me a spanking to make me stop. I guess this was the side of his character that would later play overwhelmingly large part in my upbringing.

2 - WE ARRIVE IN CANADA

It was on the 24th of July 1949 that the four of us emigrated. I was nearly three years old and my brother Jon was just two. We sailed from Liverpool on the Empress of Canada arriving a week later via the St. Lawrence River to Montreal, Quebec. We then journeyed by train across the continent to Vancouver. The days and nights on that train must have had an effect on me as I always have a feeling of nostalgia whenever I hear a train clicking over the joints with a steady rhythm and the sound of the horn with its strange, almost primeval whine. I can remember nothing of the train journey which took several days and crossed the flat of the prairies then navigated through the Rocky Mountains.

We stayed in a Vancouver hotel while a job for my father was being sorted out. It being summer, we spent a lot of time on the beach in English Bay. My mother told me she was a bit 'put out' when she was approached by a policeman while we were on the beach. She was told that it would be advisable to put some clothes on the children as it wasn't appropriate for them to be running about and playing in public while naked. She had never had that problem in England as it was acceptable there, particularly as the children were so young.

Finally, arrangements were made that we would go to a farm in the Northwest Interior of British Columbia near a place called Telkwa, a 'First Nations or Indian' term for a 'place where the two rivers meet.' The farm was located on a bend of the Bulkley River which flowed through the Bulkley Valley, about six miles from Telkwa. We moved into a two roomed log cabin which had been used as a schoolhouse, next to the Bourgon farmhouse and my father started work for Joe, a French Canadian. His wife was English, and we called her Nan. They had two granddaughters the same age as us and were the first children we got to know and play with, Joanne and Patty. Their mother, Tona, was to be my sports teacher later when I went to High School, and she was to become one of my main mentors when it came to athletics.

The cabin was very sparsely furnished, and our first beds were made with straw-filled mattresses. There was a wood burning stove with little else and of course we had an 'out-house' which was just a hole in the ground with a wooden shelter, but I don't remember much about that as I always used a potty.

Figure 2: Our First Home Photo by Mary Jane Alan 2015

That first summer was extremely hot and Jon and I played outside most of the time. One day the two of us disappeared and mother started searching and calling out. We were discovered playing by the river. Jon had waded in and was finding it difficult to stand up as he was on the edge of the current. I can remember mother's screams. That river was treacherous, and he could easily have been caught in the strong flow and dragged under. We had no idea of the danger. When my father found out, he gave us both such a spanking, that we never went near the river again.

Winter came and the weather, by contrast to the summer, was one of the coldest they had had in many years in the area. People referred to it as 'The Winter of 1949.' Everything froze including the contents of my potty. Mother had to keep the stove going all night, not only to keep us warm, but to keep the bread, which she baked every day, from freezing. She also kept a bucket of water close to the stove. Water was not on tap but had to be carried from the river or from the farm well, a difficult job in the winter when holes had to be chopped through the ice. The temperature reached minus 40 degrees Fahrenheit equal to minus 40 degrees Centigrade for a few days, which to my parents, even my Norwegian father, was exceptionally cold.

What a shock this must all have been for my mother, having to cope with such extreme temperatures with two small children needing entertaining. My father helped, of course, but he had to be out in all weathers to tend to the animals or work away at the sawmill. She didn't even have a radio to listen to in order to know what was going on the rest of the world, let alone her home in England. From her first day in Canada, she started writing letters to her father. She wrote at least once a week and often more, adding bits until the letters could be posted. Her letters turned out to be a diary of her life in Canada and her father kept every single one. This means that I have got a lot of information about myself as well, from how I was developing, what presents I wished to have sent for my birthday or for Christmas and what my school results were.

Although I have transcribed these wonderful letters they are, of course, from my mother's point of view. The information I have obtained from them has been helpful to me in establishing a timeline and to check some facts.

How often I remember seeing my mother sitting in the kitchen by the light of a coal-oil lamp, the flame flickering and casting her shadow onto the wall, her fountain pen poised for writing. I loved the smell of the ink and the sound of the pen scratching the thin pages of airmail paper. She wrote so much to her father, asking about England and the business he was in, how her relatives were doing and how everyone was getting over the war and rationing. She must have been extremely homesick in the early days, but she was no quitter and appears to have fully intended to do her best to 'make a go of it.' How tough it must have been for her particularly as we grew older, and she had more children to cope with.

3 - THE OLD HOUSE AND FARM

Forestry and farming was the mainstay of the smallholders in the area. Joe Bourgon had cattle, chickens and pigs on his acreage on the river flat. His son, Arthur, owned another farm higher up on the plateau above which eventually my parents agreed to buy. A year later we were to move to that farm with its log-cabin house originally built for a settler family in about 1915. We later referred to it as 'The Old House.' It was located about a mile from the Bourgon farm. It had four rooms, no running water, electricity, or telephone line. Mother made curtains out of flour sacks which she dyed yellow, and she also chalk-distempered all the thin cardboard-panelled walls. Our first chairs were made from cut off ends of logs and our beds were just big boxes with mattresses.

My brother and I shared the bed with a divider down the middle. This box later became a wardrobe when we were given proper sprung beds purchased from the big Eaton's catalogue. The new beds had metal frames which had been painted brown and had little pockets of paint in the angle joints which had still not dried.

Figure 3: The Old House 1950 - 1957

I loved poking my finger into the little wells of brown goo. My childhood years were spent on this farm. My parents acquired a sawmill opposite on the western side of that treacherous river. In early summer, the river would rise to about 80 metres width when in full flow from the spring melt.

The water was always very cold as the sources were from creeks high up in the mountains with their glaciers and melting snow.

We crossed the river using a raft made of barrels lashed together and attached to a cable which was either punted over of dragged using a pulley. My father eventually improved it so that one or two people could cycle it over, making it easier. There is a photo of me together with my father, younger brothers and a young man standing on the raft in the middle of the river. We had no floatation vests or other safety equipment so I hate to think what could have happened if one of us fell in. In the winter, the river froze solid so we could walk over, often following animal tracks and finding our way around mountainous lumps of ice. The crossing was located about two miles from the Old House, where a track along the river's edge led to a narrower, quieter spot.

Figure 4: Crossing to Sawmill and Slab fire

We obtained contracts to fell trees in certain sections of the forest, bring them to the sawmill and convert the logs into lumber or railway ties. Later we would get contracts to provide poles for the telephone lines.

As we grew older, we found ourselves working on the farm and in the bush more often. In the fall and winter during school holidays we would be at the sawmill packing slabs, stacking the lumber, even carrying the boards and railway ties, or sleepers, into the boxcars by lifting one each end.

The ties were far too heavy for one person and we also had to negotiate a ramp to get them up to where either our father or a hired hand would put them in place. There was a rail siding where the boxcars were left ready for us to fill, and then the train would manoeuvre into the siding to hook them up and take them to Smithers or further afield for planing or distribution.

It was quite heavy work for children, but we had some fun in our free time. We particularly liked to jump into the sawdust pile and warm our feet. We had to be careful though, for if we exposed the really hot centre, it was likely to combust and the set fire to more than just the sawdust pile. It was into this pile that I practiced my long jumps and as my brothers and I were always competing, it was good training.

Figure 5: Moen Siding, Walcott

We lived at the camp in one of the simple cabins with bunk beds, built for us and for any workers and their families.

There was a First Nation family living in one of the cabins for one summer, so we had other children to play with. Their father was a sawyer and worked in the bush felling trees as well as packing slabs or boxcar loading at the sawmill. The sound of the power-saw buzzing loudly in the forest and the scream of the saw at the mill added to the atmosphere of the camp as well as the wood-smoke from the burning slabs. The other smell that was all embracing was that of the wild cranberries. The family in the cabin also ate a lot of smoked salmon or smoked moose-meat so my memories of the place were of strong, heady, smells.

Figure 6: Diana with Old Boy

There was also a lovely glacial fed creek nearby where we would paddle and where we would bring the horse, *Old Boy*, to drink. *Old Boy* was used for pulling logs down out of the bush and I sometimes took the reins, hooked up the logs and coaxed him down to the sawmill. I loved that horse. He would often race the trains when they came through our patch and we children would wave to the driver and conductor. They sometimes threw us a bag of candy which was a special treat.

Figure 7: Burning Slabs

One fall we found ourselves still at the sawmill when we had to go back to school. This meant that we needed to use the cable to cross the river or we were sometimes rowed across.

We then had to walk to the highway along the river and up a steep hill to meet our farm road, through some bush, over a cattle grid, along the river flat and up another steep hill to catch the school bus. It made our day so much longer. Sometimes we went to the farm on our way back from school to pick up items that we forgot to take over to the 'camp' such as a change of school clothes.

It was by the sawmill that I stepped on the nail and severely damaged my foot. We were a long way from the hospital in Smithers and the difficulty of getting out from the camp meant that we struggled on with the best first aid we could find. I had my foot in a bucket of icy cold water from the creek and once dried had a large yellowy-brown patch of iodine applied to my nail wound. Luckily, we were all well inoculated against the various disease threats such as diphtheria, tetanus, and whooping cough.

We were always getting grazes and scratches as most children do. Chickenpox, measles and mumps went through the family one after the other, particularly when we went back to school after the long summer break.

Mind you, we were not the only ones to get injured. During the second summer in Canada our father caught his right forefinger in a power-saw and also nearly lost it. He had to find his way out of the bush where he was felling trees, to the railway line where he flagged down some railway workers who were there with their 'speeder.' They took him to the nearest railway station which was at a place called *Quick* so he could be taken to hospital. He had to have a splint, so this meant that he was unable to work for a week or two resulting in a loss of income as he was on a contract.

The logs on the right were rolled onto the platform using a cant-hook and a Pick. I caught my foot between the carriage and the log.

Figure 8: Sawmill - where I damaged my foot

4 - I START SCHOOL
Telkwa Superior School

My schooldays began in September 1952, a few weeks before I turned six. Located in Telkwa, and built on a ridge just above the town, it was a single-story building with a flat roof, fairly modern with a basement containing the toilet block and some lockers. There was also an annex with a pitched roof, which was the original two roomed school, and which was used for some of the lessons. I had learned how to print my own name and, on my first day, my father took me to the school and introduced me to my teacher – Miss Wood. He said my name was Diana in his Norwegian accent making the *Di* sound like *Dee* and the next thing I knew, Miss Wood made me spell my name Deannah. The teacher was put right, however and I was allowed to spell my name the correct way. A small thing, I know, but it is one that is never forgotten. He also found a girl about my age and asked if she would look out for me. I remember she was Dutch.

The population in the Bulkley Valley was made up of many immigrants from Europe and beyond. We were Norwegian/English and there were many from Switzerland, Poland, The Netherlands, England, Scotland and Ireland and other Eastern European countries. A melting pot of cultures to add to the First Nations' People who we had as neighbours, all aiming to be Canadians. We sang 'God Save the Queen' at assembly each morning as well as 'Oh Canada.' Even in the cinema in Smithers, a town 16 miles from our farm, we all stood to listen to 'God Save the Queen' before the film began.

I would walk from the Old House to the main road to catch the yellow and black school bus. It was around two miles, the first quarter being down a steep hill to the river flat the middle along past the Bourgon farm, then the other quarter up another steep hill and along the gravel road to the main highway. I was one of the last ones to get on the bus along the route which meant that after school I was one of the last ones to get off. These turned out to be exceedingly long days.

Extract from my mother's letters: December 1953

Dear Dad,
We are all very well and Freda is growing fast. The weather is turning colder now, and we have had about 6 inches of snow. Your Christmas cards have already arrived, and the children were very pleased with these. Diana read them out to Jon and Paul. She manages the long walk to school every day much better this year and comes home in the dark nights and doesn't mind at all. I used to go to meet her last year, but I can't this year with the baby, but she is so grown-up in her ways now and likes to be independent.

In winter, I would set off to school in the dark and arrive home in the dark. At first, my father accompanied me, but it was not long before I had to walk alone. The farm was really in the wilderness with the wildlife all around. My trek to the highway was through bear, cougar, wolf, moose, deer, and coyote country. I obviously survived.

Occasionally I would walk along the highway, about two hundred yards from our road turning to where a neighbour's boy, Roy, waited for the bus, so I had some company. He was often late as he could see the bus from his house so ran up his lane while everyone watched. Once the roads became icy the bus could be late so, to while away the time, we would play grownups and discuss what our house would be like when we got married. We would place twigs down in a cleared snow patch indicating where the kitchen, bedrooms and front room would be. We didn't give a thought to the 'outhouse' as we hadn't yet learned to expect an indoor toilet.

Roy's parents had a farm with livestock and Roy would often be seen sitting precariously on top of a cart full of hay, pulled by his father with his tractor to and from a meadow by the river next to our place. We were not the only children who had to work when not going to school.

That walk up the road was full of adventures for me. I loved to poke at the ice on the puddles and watch the melting ice and snow forming rivulets on the big hill up out of river flat. At the top of the hill there was a thicket with a small pond and there were often birds called chickadees chirping away in the shrubs. I would spend a lot of time trying to *'chickadeedeedee'* like them.

Another time when I was walking home along the flat, I had wandered over to the base of the hill and spied my brother's braces. They were colourful with stripes. I thought he had lost them and that he would be pleased I had found them, so I bent down to pick them up and got the shock of my life. It was a snake that shot out of my grasp. I was told later that it was a garter snake and quite harmless.

I scared my mother on the day I discovered where some beautiful *lady's slipper* orchids grew and thought I would pick them for my teacher. I spent so much time searching at the base of the hill on the way home, that she started to walk down the hill to find me. I had lost all idea of time and was so absorbed in finding these gems in the moss that she had become worried. I didn't know then that the flowers wouldn't last five minutes once picked and that they might be considered rare. There was also a small cabin, probably a playhouse near the orchid patch hidden by the poplar and birch trees. I did enjoy dawdling sometimes but I probably scooted home much faster after that incident. My mother was not too happy with me.

Further along the highway was the last bus-stop where there

were several houses near to each other belonging to the extended family of Thomas and Mary George, both hereditary First Nation chiefs from different clans. They were living off-reservation and several of their grandchildren were friends of ours.

Some days, as the bus wound up the hill, we would find ourselves above the clouds and below we only saw fog, but we could still see the snow-covered peek of Hudson Bay Mountain and the Telkwa Range in the distance. The bus then continued on around a rural route which included Round Lake and Quick returning to the Yellowhead Highway 16, before descending into Telkwa and up the gravelled road to our school.

Our school playground was rather rough and was also gravelled so when we fell and grazed our knees, we knew about it. In the winter, the hill up to the school was often icy and there was a small ski slope above the school ending in the playground. We also played baseball and at the recess bell, or after our lunch, we would all rush out crying 'First up Second up. Pitcher' and formed ourselves into teams, usually mixed and all of different ages. There are so many little stories I could tell you here about my early days at the school, one such was when there was a skunk under the old annex. It seemed to be trapped there for ages and my goodness it was pungent. There was also a time when there was a lot of hilarity when one of our teachers slipped on the icy slope outside the school and we all got to see her 'bloomers.'

It was during one of those baseball breaks that I tripped over first base in my effort to get there as quick as I could and ended up with graze full of gravel and a scar for life. However, I proved myself one day when a very tall Dutch boy called Henry was pitching the ball to me. I think I missed the first ball, and he came much closer, gave me an overly soft underhand pitch and I whacked it right into his nose. I felt terrible of course, seeing the blood and what I had done. I don't think anyone who saw it happen ever sent me a soft, gentle ball again.

As I was English and had an English accent, which I really didn't want at school, I misunderstood the meaning of Canadian words. One particular time, when a girl told my teacher that it was me who had scrawled my name on the wall, which I hadn't because it was spelled 'Dianne,' I insisted that it wasn't me. When the teacher said, 'you are lying little girl,' I retaliated by saying that I was standing so I was then accused of being 'cheeky.' If only I had known what 'lying' meant. Being shy and very much an introvert did not help me very much. The headmaster actually had 'the strap' held up ready to strike my hand but for some reason he must have thought better of it and let me go.

I remember several incidences of boys being given the strap and I guess sometimes some form of punishment had to be given if detention wasn't enough, but it did cause a lot of distress and I found the thought extremely frightening. I had a friend who had a naughty brother and when he got the strap, she became almost hysterical and I often tried to console her. I did have a memorable detention myself once where I had to stay and write lines in my recess. I couldn't stay after school as I had to catch the one and only bus home, but it was punishment anyway. It was from an incident when all the children who couldn't go home for lunch because they came from rural areas, had to sit at desks in one particular classroom so we could be monitored while we ate our sandwiches. I had long braids and a boy called Gordon thought it would be fun to dunk one of my braids into an inkwell. I was cross and upset and told the teacher who challenged Gordon. He denied it. For some reason, the teacher believed Gordon and not me and I had to write 'I will not be a tell lies' or words to that effect. I can still smell the ink from those ink wells and the rubber from our erasers as well as the chalk we used on the blackboards. I hated the scratchy sound of chalk on those boards which I am reminded of whenever I visit the dentist.

My report cards from Telkwa school were perhaps not particularly exciting and gave my parents no cause for any great concern. I was 'conscientious,' I was 'a pleasure to teach and have in the class,' and 'the whole class enjoyed my 'morning news.' My behaviour was good, but it ended there. I wonder what my news was about. I was a 'very quiet student who speaks in a low voice.' I'm still surprised to this day that no one questioned why I was such an introvert. I'm also surprised that when I drew a picture of an erect penis on the blackboard for a friend who asked me what a boy's private parts looked like, it wasn't detected. Either my friend didn't tell her mother or, if she did, it wasn't believed, or we made a good job of erasing it. I find it strange that I can so distinctly remember that incident, too.

There are many little snippets that I remember from time to time when something jogs my memory. One uncomfortable one was of the plight of an overweight girl with large breasts and a sleek, dark 'bob.' The boys always seemed to be teasing her and there was a time when one of them took the stapler and stapled her bum. It was a terrible thing to do in my eyes, but I think I was quite reluctant to tell on anyone even though I was upset at having witnessed it. I guess it was a form of bullying which I didn't realize was happening at the time. I don't remember the outcome.

So, there were bad times but there were also fun times. Halloween when we had a bonfire and celebrations at the school which we attended with our parents was one of the most exciting events of the year. We all got dressed up and bundled up because it was often very cold, then the family drove to town and up to park in the playground, the windscreen would often be smeared with soap or candlewax or something sticky and horrible, even as we were queueing to park, much to our mother's annoyance. There was a lot of tricks or treating going on too. Potatoes in foil were put into the fire and we roasted wieners and marshmallows on sticks. Candy was also available in abundance which was a particular treat for us as having anything sweet was frowned upon by my father. We all stood outside the school with masks and various ghoulish costumes to watch the firework display put on by the fire department. I always thought they were fired out of a cannon placed at the top of the hill above Telkwa and it was quite a lovely sight with all the sparkling colours showering out above the river and the two bridges with the dark bush and mountains in the background.

Excitement continued the next day when we returned to school. Some of the pupils were being punished for having done some amazing, often dangerous tricks but in our eyes, they just seemed to have been having naughty fun. Whole toilets, which were wooden structures outside in those days, would have been tipped over. I remember that some boys had even managed to put a teacher's car onto a roof of a shed and invariably the school windows had been daubed with sticky glue or soap and toilet paper had been strewn all over the playground.

As you may guess, I loved going to school. I would not miss a day for anything and even though I had the long walk, I managed to attend school every day for about five years. It wasn't until I caught flu or yellow jaundice that I had to stay home. I just did not want to miss out and besides, I didn't wish to stay home on my own if my father was inside while my mother was out doing chores. My grades were reasonably good as well and I had some excellent teachers, particularly Miss Thran whom we all loved.

5 - I Go to Highschool
Smithers High School

In September 1960 when I was nearly 14, I started high school in Smithers full time. This meant that I caught the bus to Telkwa and then we journeyed on to Smithers, a distance of about 16 miles.

As I had wished to go to University after High school, I took the appropriate courses as well as Commerce, which included typing, and Home Economics. As there were too many pupils taking French, I had to delay that until the following year and when I did, I was taught by a German teacher. We all thought that was fun and I suppose he had to put up with a lot from us. Chemistry was also a subject I enjoyed, especially as we had to have partners to do the experiments with and my ones were Diana Hann and Judy Calderwood. Again, the teacher we had was Mr. Todd and he always seemed strict, telling us to 'burn that midnight oil,' and 'if you wish to commit suicide, do it somewhere far away. I don't want to be scraping jam off the sidewalk.' He was a memorable character, but I did learn my periodic tables and it helped later in life when I needed to understand about formulas for farm chemicals and fertilizers.

I became passionate about school but there was a lot of homework and with all the books I had to carry back and forth, I guess I was doing 'resistance' training for my sports.

Figure 9: Visiting friends in Smithers - Shy teenager

We had a horse racetrack in Smithers, which we simply called 'The track-field,' not far from the school and it was there that I did most of my distance training with my teachers, Tona Heatherington and Miss Oyama who was Japanese. We had high jump and long jump pits into sawdust as well and if I had to stay late to do extra practice, my mother would often come and fetch me as there was no second bus.

I remember taking part in one 220 yards race around that The Track and because it was so rough one of my spikes got caught in a piece of wood from a fallen branch. I had to stop to take it off. I was more than upset as I had been well ahead at that point but only managed to finish second or third. However, I had a huge amount of encouragement from my teachers and I really thought that if I went south to Vancouver, I would be able to train for national and international events. We were a small town, but I had plenty of competition and we did have track meets between the other towns in the interior such as Terrace, Hazleton and Burns Lake. The main one was called The Northwest Interior Track Meet and one year I tied for first place with Alice Williams by getting first in four disciplines (Long jump, 100 yards, 220 yards and relay) and she obtained hers in four other disciplines. For a few years I held the school record for long jump.

My school report cards give a bit of a picture as to how I coped. During the first years at Telkwa Elementary aged 6 to 10, I had quite a few days off due to either the very cold weather in January and February when even the school closed, or if I had become too ill. There were also times when we were kept off to help on the farm during some difficult periods with the cattle. However, when I went to Smithers, I attended every day for 4 years without missing a single one. The two main reasons that I refused to stay home unless I had to was that I did not want to miss any of my friends, and I did not want to stay at home ill in case I was left alone with my father.

I gave both my parents a fright when I came home with my results one year. I had made a good grade, perhaps it was an 'A' but on the way home I managed to convince myself that I had failed miserably so that when I got home, I presented a very glum face. In fact, I think I was almost in tears, so it was with some difficulty that I managed to snap myself out of it when I revealed the truth. Perhaps they might have guessed anyway but I felt bad about having tried to pretend that I had done badly.

My schoolwork was generally satisfactory, and I sometimes received an A or two, a few Bs and C+s but during the last year at High School when things were getting ever more difficult at home, my schoolwork deteriorated rapidly. I did however receive an award for my athletics as well as a lovely big S shaped badge for sport to put on my basketball jacket and a big C for citizenship which I kept in a folder. My desire to go to university was shattered of course and when I received my final results, sent to me in England, I was only awarded 95 credits where I had needed 120 credits to qualify for entrance. I would have had to repeat my last year.

Figure 10: Athletics 1961 - 4 Firsts and Trophy

6 – THE WEATHER AND ITS INFLUENCES

As the weather got colder, we experienced problems with the bus getting up the icy hill and the ice and cold caused some strange problems. My friend called Heather was standing beside me by the metal rail leading down the steps to the toilet block which was indoors in the basement of the school. It was the elementary school in Telkwa, so I was about nine years old. It was bitterly cold, and it was necessary to hold on to the rails to avoid slipping on the icy steps. Our damp mittens were caked in ice. For some reason Heather decided to stick out her tongue to taste the frost. Her tongue got stuck fast to the rail and we didn't know just what to do. I knew that if we had a band-aid or plaster stuck on our skin, the quicker it was pulled off the less it hurt. I held her and we pulled. She came unstuck but, my goodness, did I ever feel guilty as she screamed in pain. She obviously recovered but I don't know what an adult would have done in the circumstances. I don't remember ever being reprimanded or told I shouldn't have helped her that way. I guess it was just one of those many little accidents that happen to children in the playground. We both learned a good lesson that day anyway.

The fact that I had to walk over two miles each way every day probably helped with my fitness and as I got older, I would often break into a run. In the winter we would sometimes ski to the highway and leave the skis behind a snowbank so we could ski home again. There were also times when the road was so blocked with chest-deep snow that I took turns with my brother, who joined me for school by my third year, to forge a path in front in order to make it to the road. Sometimes, when the temperature was well below zero, perhaps as much as minus 32 degrees Fahrenheit and if the school was open, we would have to bundle up with newspapers lining our over-boots, scarves over our noses, double mittens, woollen toque and earmuffs before setting off. We were told to watch each other's noses in case of frost bite. If the temperature got much lower, the water pipes at the school would freeze and school was not open. Because we had no telephone, we sometimes found ourselves at the highway waiting until the bus driver, who had to be the messenger, went around the route to tell us to return home. The coldest I remember was minus 40 degrees Fahrenheit and we definitely did not go to school then.

Figure 11: Ploughing deep snow with horses

At that time, girls were not allowed to wear trousers or slacks, so I had to wear a skirt over top of my trousers and then take them off at school. During the first year my mother managed to persuade the authorities to let me wear trousers, but later on I had to wear a skirt or dress, whatever the weather. Tights had not been invented so I had the added discomfort of having to wear stockings held up with a garter belt that fitted over my shoulders and of course when I reached puberty, I had the monthly discomfort of wearing a thick, leg-chafing towel affixed with a belt around my waist. It made for a painful walk sometimes.

The roads in winter were treacherous. We often had great difficulty in driving up the hill from the river flat to our farm as well and often made little headway, even on foot. When there was a thaw and sudden freeze, it was a matter of 'putting one foot forward and taking two steps back' according to my mother. We had to have winter chains on the tyres of the car but even then, we sometimes had to leave it at the bottom of the hill. I can remember my mother having to take several goes and move through the gears very efficiently in order to get up.

There was one incident I remember particularly well. My mother had been to collect us children from school as she was in town on business. The car was loaded up with flour and eggs and a few other groceries. As she was driving around a bend in the highway between our neighbours' entrances, the Georges and the Goheens, a car was coming in the opposite direction. There was a crash and it set all us children off crying and screaming. Luckily, no-one was hurt, and we were taken to the Goheens while the police came and dealt with the accident. The other driver admitted liability which was relief to our mother and the kind policeman took us home, flour, eggs, and all. The car had to be towed away. To my mind it was a most horrific happening and one I would never forget.

I learned a lot from these experiences so that when it was my turn to drive, I was able to cope with the icy conditions fairly well. In fact, the day I took my driving test, we had had a 'chinook' and there were black-ice patches in many places just off the highway where they hadn't put any salt down.

Keeping track of the temperature in both summer and winter kept us children constantly amused. When we got onto the school bus, there would be a discussion as to who had the coldest or hottest recording. From our farm above the river, we descended to the river flat and the temperature would drop by several degrees. As we climbed back up at the other end, in winter the sun would warm our backs and by the time we got to the top we were very warm. However, when we got the highway, we were cold again. How often I remember comparing notes. 'It was minus 32 degrees at our place'. 'Oh, it was minus 40 at our place' then in summer it would be: 'Hey, it was 90 degrees at lunch time yesterday at our place'. 'Well, it was 95 degrees at ours!'. In fact, for a few days each summer we had extremely hot weather and the fun started when someone said they had cooked their eggs on the bonnet of their car. We did get extreme conditions in the valley, but we could never beat the amazing temperatures of the areas further south such as in Caribou country. Inevitably someone had heard the forecast from a cousin or friend who lived in another part of British Columbia who boasted of knowing the high temperatures. In July it would be: 'It was 110 degrees in Kamloops' or, in January, the opposite: 'It was minus 45 degrees in Prince George.'

We had one or two summers where the weather was exceptionally dry and hot resulting in huge forest fires. It was part of the curriculum to have lessons about the fires, and I made a poster of one which went up on the classroom wall. I felt proud of it and remember working with the colours in order to get the flames as bright as possible with oranges and yellows. It was a warning: 'Prevent Forest Fires. Don't throw cigarette butts out of car windows.'

The worst fires I experienced happened in the summer of 1958 when I was 12 years old. There was so much smoke in the valley that it made the sun appear red. Any burning of the slabs at the sawmill was forbidden and all available people in area had to go to help particularly those who had bull dozers to help make firebreaks.

Figure 12: Mother on sandbank with 3 of us 1952

Floods were frequent in the valley too. When the snows melted up in the mountains there would be a huge amount of water coming down at once. The river became a raging torrent capable of bringing down bridges and we would watch in awe as we saw whole trees with even their roots still attached, sweeping down with gathered detritus in front of them. Occasionally there would be odd items and carcasses of cattle or moose, but mostly it would be lumber and logs. It could be quite frightening to observe, and we felt lucky to have our farm so high up on the plateau.

7 - NEIGHBOURS

Being so isolated, we children didn't spend much time playing with neighbours so most of our contact was either on the school bus or at school during recess. During the summer holidays most of our time was spent on the farm either helping or playing and exploring in the woods and fields around the house. Sometimes we would be outside all day and only come in when called to lunch or supper.

We did have neighbours with children our age and sometimes we would attend parties at their homes, or they might come to play with us if my parents invited their families for a picnic or a wiener roast. We made a few excursions as a family to the lake north of Telkwa called Tyhee or Maclure Lake and of course there were yearly events at Round Lake.

When my father was away, my mother organized for us to join a square-dancing club at a place called Quick where there was a church and community centre. I really enjoyed the dancing and I even got to dance in a competition at Burns Lake. My dancing partner was Ian Meiklem, and I was friendly with his sister Sheelagh. Later on in life, when I was living in London, England, Sheelagh and I shared an apartment for a few months. The outfits we wore for the dance is fixed in my memory.

My mother made a full circle skirt for herself and me that matched. It whirled out when I spun and revealed a crinoline underneath. It was in a brown patterned material which was teamed with a white blouse. The men and boys, including my brother Jon, wore shirts to match the skirts. I was even allowed to wear my first pair of clip-on earrings which really hurt but I persevered with them.

We practiced at the church or community hall at Quick and then sometimes joined in the square dances and barn dances held at Round Lake Hall. I always enjoyed the square dances when a particular 'caller' would guide us through our steps with his unusual voice. Unfortunately, I do not remember his name.

Other neighbours included the Sundins whose entrance to their road met ours nearly at the end just before the highway. One of the boys was quite naughty and I remember they had some pigs including a sow and Ralph used to tease the poor animal by poking her with stick. I picked a fight with him once as I hated seeing what he did to her. However, my brother was angry with me because I 'threw his friend into the ditch.'

I mentioned the Goheens before and Roy had a sister called Gwen. She was younger than me, but we would meet up a short way from her house. I would walk nearly to her place, and she would come via a short-cut across a field to meet me. We called ourselves a 'club' and made a badge each and planned a newsletter. I was always fascinated by a ring Gwen had which had the whole Lords' Prayer under a piece of magnifying glass. I couldn't believe how small it could be and still be readable. We exchanged gifts as well and I still have a little pedant with a hare embossed on it which she gave me. I had a lot of fun planning the newsletter as I wanted to write articles and put poems in it, however our friendship faded when I went to High School and she was also a lot younger than me.

Roy, on the other hand remained a friend. I was upset when I heard that he had to have a regular spanking with a strap from his father every Saturday whether he had done anything naughty or not. Perhaps it was a family tradition. Roy was also very industrious. He collected the beer bottles that were flung out of cars all along the highway and made his pocket money that way. When the truck arrived from the Okanagan loaded with watermelons, he was always waiting to be first in the line for some. I don't know if he sold them on, but I do remember the scramble to be at the right place in Telkwa when the truck arrived.

The Bourgon farm which we passed by on our way up the road and which was about a mile away from our home was sold to the Redman family, so we called it The Redmans. They had children all younger than me, so I didn't personally have much to do with them other than babysitting and helping with their mother's ironing. In fact, my first paid job was ironing those clothes for Maryanne while she was pregnant. I also became involved in feeding their dog, Lassie when they were away on holiday. Lassie had control over me because one day on my way home from school I gave her one of my sandwiches so that my mother thought I had eaten all my lunch. Lassie realized then that if she came to me and bared her teeth, I would give her a piece of whatever I had left in my lunch box. It got to the point that I so fearful of her that I actually saved my sandwiches to be able to get past her. The only sandwiches I really wanted to eat were jam ones. Perhaps I liked the colour as well as the sweetness because at one time I would only eat my mashed potatoes if they were pink from mashing beetroot in with them. I often swapped my good homemade bread sandwiches with a friend who always came to school with Angel cake. I guess she got the better deal.

One day Maryanne asked if I would like to go to Smithers with her and her latest baby. It was fun for me to get an opportunity to go shopping. We were driving down the high street past the pool hall when suddenly a man with blood running down his face, opened the car door and tried to push Maryanne across to the passenger side so he could drive. He was trying to run away from the police. Maryanne was luckily wearing high heel shoes and she stabbed at his feet with them and somehow managed to get him to let go. It was a very scary incident but was over quickly. I do not remember the outcome but I do know her high-heels and her bravery saved us.

My younger brothers and sisters became very friendly with the Redman children however, and in winter we often went over to their side of the fence where there was a good ski slope to go skiing and sledding down. It was the perfect place for a toboggan party too, just out of sight of our own house.

Our other neighbours were members of a First Nation clan or band, a couple of whom did work for my father, helping to build our New House as well felling trees in the bush for our sawmill. Frederick and Andrew George, young men who were veterans of WW2 having played their part on the battlefields of Europe. One of them had a couple of cows and asked for payment in hay. They didn't have enough cleared land themselves to make the necessary amount of hay to carry them through the winter themselves, though they did have an area for grazing. I remember Freddy as being quite tall and seemingly happy and friendly. Bartering was still used a lot in payment during the time that we were living in the valley.

Ruby Thomas, who may have been a cousin of the indigenous family and who lived with the George's became a friend to me and I was fascinated by the fact she had blue eyes but dark hair. I would save her a place beside me on the bus. One of the Georges' daughters called Jacky was quite different, and I always felt she hated me, probably because of my friendship with Ruby. We were all neighbours, and I don't remember giving any thought to our differences until I was much older and became aware of the history and struggles of the indigenous families in our area. The Georges were the last on and the first to get off the bus that clambered slowly up the big hill behind their homes. The houses were on either side of the road and at the entrance to the main family home was a set of totem poles. Unfortunately, when I visited the area many years later, the totem poles were gone.

I always felt proud that I was friends with the Georges while we went to school at Telkwa. They were involved in all the school activities. A couple of sisters were excellent singers and I always thought that one of the boys looked like Elvis Presley. I cannot remember his name, but he played the guitar. Another boy, Ronnie, who was a year older than me was friendly with my brother. I remember he was one of the top students in his class. However, once I moved on to High School in Smithers, I lost touch with them. They may have already moved away by then.

I later learned that Thomas George was from the Gisdayway clan and his wife Mary George was from the Tsaybaysa clan. Their hereditary lands covered many thousands of hectares and was known as Wet'suwet'en. A part of our farm was at a place called Hubert which was on part of their territory. Of course, I had no idea about this during the time we lived there except that I understood that Thomas George was chief of the Bear Clan. Several of their grandchildren were my classmates. I learned later that although Freddy and Andy George were an integral part of the Canadian forces and served in France, they were not recognized as other service men and women were so didn't receive medals until around 1962. It was through the great efforts and nearly life-long lobbying by their nephew Ron that they got some recognition. I mention this because I have known Ron as a friend for a long time.

I had several friends who lived in Telkwa but saw them only at school. One was Jill, the daughter of the pharmacist who had the Telkwa Drugstore. Another was Mary Jane Langevin who became a good friend and with whom I remained in touch. There were also a couple of Dutch girls, Alice Gerzema who was good at sports and one of my competitors and Jenny Veenstra whose cousin worked for us on the farm for a few summers. I met up with some of them years later when we had a re-union for the class of 1964 from Smithers' High School. Sheelagh Meiklem who lived much further away from Telkwa and had to walk more than the two miles than I had to walk in order to catch the bus became another friend.

The fact that the population was so diverse in ethnic origins meant that we joined together for many events. One family who lived further down the river from us near to Smithers and the Smithers' Bridge, were ardent theatre goers and they often held plays on their land to which we were invited. They had a hill above their property which was fashioned into an Amphitheatre.

We always called them The Thens. They had children our age and my mother sometimes found herself in hospital having her baby at the same time as Marjorie Then who was also English. Her husband, Tadek was Polish with a long Polish surname that was shortened. I became good friends with their daughter Vanda who was the same age as me and we have remained in contact. It was good to have something in common with another family going through similar trials and tribulations as us. I sometimes think of ourselves as 'mid-century' pioneers - perhaps a second wave of settlers from Europe.

The sawmill and bush work kept my father busy, but we also had the farm which gave my mother a lot of work combined with coping with us children. We had about 60 head of polled Hereford beef cattle with pasture for them as well as fields for growing crops. This meant that the land had to be tilled and harvested. I learned to drive the Grey Ferguson tractor by the time I was thirteen, and you would have seen me mowing hay, raking it into rows and then helping with the baling. It was also hard work, just as at the sawmill. Before we got the baler, the hay was still being put into hay stooks which was eventually carted to a haystack. When we had a crop of oats, a neighbour who owned a combine harvester, would come under contract and there was great excitement because he had a daughter about my age. However, most of our crops were of alfalfa, timothy and clover so the harvest was a time of lovely grassy smells.

The worst job I had occurred when we acquired the baler. Sometimes, if the hay was too damp, the bales would come out very compacted and this would put pressure on the tying machine. This meant that the tension caused the knotter to fail, and my job was to sit on the back of the baler, adjust the tension, and as each bale that came through without a knot, I would have to tie one very quickly before the bale reached the end of the chute. I certainly knew how not to make a 'Granny' knot. I had to wear a scarf around my mouth and nose because of the dust and bits of chaff. I looked a real sight with a black dusty face and only the whites of my eyes blinking above the scarf. The itching of the chaff was horrible. My brothers had the job of putting the bales onto a raft being dragged behind the baler and it was very tough for them too, in all the dust.

It was especially difficult for them if I failed to tie the knot and the bales burst sending hay or straw everywhere. Sometimes the haymaking went on well into the night if the weather was going to turn and when we contracted another acreage a few miles from home, I remember coming back well after midnight. What a welcome relief it was when the machinery broke down. It meant that mother had to drive into town to order or pick up a part and we had a few days off. No doubt some other tasks was found for us in the interim.

Figure 13: My brothers carrying heavy bales

When we first started to set up and bought a few cattle, the electric fence had not been completed. My brother and I had to take turns taking a day off school to check that the cows didn't stray. It wasn't a bad job as I loved the cows and I also liked to lick their blocks of salt which probably wasn't a good idea. They were either red or blue depending on the minerals the cattle needed. It was also fun to be able to call them so they would come running. I would have been eight years old then and Jon seven. However, the crops of clover had recently been planted and needed to be protected. Later I helped with the fencing with barbed wire from a huge prickly roll a stapled to posts that had been soaked in a blue liquid called copper sulphate. We also had an electric fence which I always tried to avoid but of course my father couldn't let me get away without finding out what it felt like to grab hold of the live wire. It was a horrible sensation and I absolutely detested doing it. Obviously, the current wasn't enough to kill a cow but enough to stop her trying to break through and it certainly worked on me.

Another little job we had was that of picking rocks. We were given buckets and had to collect the rocks that sprang to the surface after the spring thaw and put them in piles. It was a tedious task and one time I remember we decided that as we were over the brow of the hill and out of sight, we could just sit by the pile and throw rocks onto it so it sounded as though we were working. We were soon found out, however.

Being so isolated on our farm during the summer holidays we rarely saw any other children. If a stranger came up the road, we all got extremely excited. Occasionally we would have visitors, especially when we had a birthday to celebrate and were allowed to invite some friends. We were also fascinated if someone drove up wearing smart suit and carrying a brief case because it would usually mean we were being paid a visit by a Jehovah's Witness. They were usually politely told by my parents that we were not interested. I was always intrigued with the literature they left behind for us to peruse but the little booklets and leaflets would disappear before I had read through much of them. However, there was once a visit by a rather large, overweight lady and I think my mother felt sorry for her so invited her in for a cup of tea. It certainly gave us all something to talk about afterwards.

Christmas was a good time because we were often invited to a party at The Wearne's, an English couple who had arrived after the First World War. Harry had a metal plate in his head from having been injured in Alsace Lorraine and could not tolerate the smell of candles burning. It reminded him of the smell of cordite. He seemed so old to us. His wife Hilary liked everything English and had a very English garden with holy-hocks, Russel Lupins and English roses. All her guests seemed to be from England too and we all loved going to their house which was even farther away from 'civilization' than us. I remember I did a school project called 'Old-timers of the Interior' which involved an interview with Harry and later on, when I lived in London, England, I met him for lunch. He was over on holiday to see the gorillas at Regents Park Zoo. I think he preferred animals to people, but he was an interesting character and I held him in high regard.

Harry also made beautiful animal carvings which he displayed at the Round Lake summer fair which we would attend as a family. The name for the lake was most apt as it was an almost perfect circle. There was a community hall there where people from all around would gather to dance and have meetings. Sometimes there would be a contemporary band playing the 50s songs and other times there would be a barn dance or a square dance with accordions and fiddles. Lumberjacks would often turn up to dance in their heavy boots but there were also those who came wearing a Stetson hat and cowboy boots. The ladies' dresses were often quite full and when I was in my teens, I felt very grown up wearing a fawn-coloured shirtwaist dress with a crinoline. It was made from a brocade material embossed with tiny Chinese temples. I loved that dress until a drunken man reached around behind me when I was sitting with my mother on a bench. I felt a sudden sharp pain in my bottom and discovered he had burnt a hole in my dress with his cigarette. I was terribly upset and just couldn't wait to go home. I was already feeling like a 'wall flower' anyway and this was just the end. It is strange how some little incident can become a big issue. It confirmed to me that I was an outsider and it made me feel even more like withdrawing into myself.

The fair often had a merry-go-round as well as some stalls with 'toss the ring' and a 'coconut shy.' One time I spun the ring and managed to hook a prize, but I was to be disappointed when I wasn't given the big teddy bear, but a small pearl handled penknife instead. It was the first time that I felt cheated. However, I kept the penknife along with my small collection of keepsakes. All the families brought rugs and a picnic and there would be stalls for hot-dogs, cakes or ice-cream. Organized games were always fun, but I never tried the 'greased pole' though my brothers did. Our neighbour, Thomas George, would be there with his children and grand-children too and he would often put on his colourful blanket and head-dress to give us a display of his clan's dancing. In fact, there were many people from the various ethnic communities mixing together and enjoying the summer fair.

So, along with other local artwork which included items such as embroidered moccasins, beaded bands, knitwear, paintings and carvings, there were Harry Wearne's intricately carved deer and moose. Sadly, after he died, their house burnt down, and all his carvings were destroyed.

As we got older, we would venture further afield to visit neighbours, particularly during school holidays and could be gone from home for most of the day, returning before dark. In order to do so, we would have to take the only road out which passed by the original log cabin we first lived in. I don't have many memories of actually living in it as I was so young but later, having found out that it had been a school at one time, we plucked up the courage to explore the loft only to find loads of books and school registers. I was fascinated with the names in the registers as they turned out to be the parents of some of my friends. Among the names were: Jimmy, Fred and Andy George, Bolithos and Forsyths. We felt that we were trespassers which made it all the more exciting. Obviously while we were living there, we had no idea what was above the ceiling. I felt we had found a gold mine when leafing through the books. There was one on art with glossy pictures of the colour wheel and how to make shades and hues but, better still, there were some poetry books. One anthology had 'The Purple Cow' by *Gelett Burgess* in it. I learned that poem by heart and loved to recite it. It was finding those books that probably influenced me to write to my grandfather saying that I wanted to be a poet when I grew up. As to poetry, my mother also had a little book of poems by Robert Browning which I spent time trying to decipher. I was also fascinated by the colour-wheel and the way that colours complimented each other, however this fascination never led me to become an artist.

Schoolhouse - Abandoned Circa 1939

On the flat land by the river,

preserved in its isolation,

a log house with timber slates

melts into the landscape.

Two rooms only, with porch and loft,

In one room, a black iron stove,

stovepipe bent to an outlet in the wall.

The other is bare to its board-wood floor,

apart from some scattered acorn shells.

In the shallow loft - books.

Registers with names,

dates, attendances and absences,

ticks and crosses inked in red and green -

Fredrick, Andrew and Jimmy G

Johan, Peter and Janet B

essays still await a teacher's comment.

Books of poems about purple cows.

Books of fables and tales of Paul Bunyan.

Books by Browning and Keats and Masefield.

Books on painting, mathematics, science.

Abandoned to a new school down-river.

11.07.05

9- I START TO RUN

My very first race was in the playground at Telkwa School. A line was drawn for the start and we were told to run a straight line to the end. It was probably no more than about 60 yards. My mother stood among the other parents when my group of six-year-olds were given the instructions: 'On your marks. Get set. Go!' and I set off as fast as I could over the rough ground. I heard someone shout 'Break the tape Diana' so what did I do? I stopped and tried to break the tape.

How I looked forward to sports day as I got older when we could set off from home in shorts and T shirt in the colours of our houses. I belonged to House 3, whose colour was yellow, so we had T shirts to match and to make it more exciting our houses were named after animals, and I proudly took part for the Wolverines. 'One, two, three, four, who are we for, house three, house three rah, rah, rah.' I won trophies and ribbons right up to and through high school, my main events being sprinting the 100 and 220 yards as well as long jump. Luckily, I had the farm to practice on and often went for long runs around the fence-line and along tracks in the forest adjoining our land. I would don my spikes when running down along the river flat. I also enjoyed games and was in the Smithers High School basketball team. Baseball and ice hockey eluded me as we didn't live near enough to town to join in when I was younger, and it was only when I went to Smithers' High School that I joined the basketball and volleyball teams.

One time, when I entered a long open cross-country race which was held the Telkwa BBQ, I came in well ahead of some girls who were much older than me. They complained and said I had cheated. How I cannot imagine as the field was visible to everyone. However, my mother persuaded the organizers to allow us to race again. Unfortunately for them, I won again so there was no doubt.

Extract from my mother's letters to her father in June 1961. Age 14.

"All this about the house and I've not mentioned the children's sports yet. This year is Diana's triumph. It's the first year at High School and she won the cup at the Inter High School Sports. She won all races she entered and some of them were 'open,' so she was running against 18-year-olds. She shared the honour with another girl, an excellent high jumper, while Diana is the best runner and broad jumper. It was a nice experience for her as she not only won for herself but won honours for her school, as her points of course helped Smithers to win most points over the other two schools. She is best at 220 yards and in every race when she has a long enough distance, she comes racing out amazingly far ahead of all the others, it's really exciting to watch her."

The freedom I experienced when running around the fence-line along the ridge above the river was rewarding. There was a spring where I would often stop as it fascinated me how water would just appear out of the ground. There were also some tiny creatures encased in a crust which lived just where the water dribbled out and my imagination ran wild. I thought I had discovered something quite alien and it became a secret place.

Also along the ridge were ant hills which had to be avoided, particularly after my brother decided that an ant hill might make a good seat for a king to sit on. I remember seeing his face and how his eyes stared out when he suddenly realized, he was being bitten and became covered in the black and red devils. He was lucky that there was help to brush them off but a sting from one of those ants was very painful.

Cross country running and skiing became my lifeline.

9 - THE LIVING WASN'T EASY

Life on the farm was basic and simple. It was very much a make do and mend way for us. Our father was always coming up with ideas and starting projects that would all cost money, so we relied very heavily on money given or lent from our mother's father. She had inherited money from her grandparents and also had shares in her father's business. This meant that we were continuously being bailed out of debt.

The idea of acquiring some horses became an issue for my parents. I was about thirteen at the time. Our father thought it would be a great idea and no doubt us children encouraged him. The thought of being real cowboys was appealing. I expect my mother knew a bit about how much work is involved in looking after them. He eventually persuaded her, and the subject discussed endlessly for several months was finally concluded. So, we went for a two-week trip to Vancouver, our first real holiday. We had a panelled van at that time which had windows put in and alterations were made to fit it out so we could sleep in the back. I think we did have a tent, but I remember there being canvas camp bunks in it. I experienced carsickness as well and found that I could overcome it if I nibbled on crab-apples, some of which were found when we pulled in and camped along the way.

The expedition, for that is what it became, was to be not only our summer holiday but it was also a chance to get some proper dental work done as we were short of a dentist in the valley at the time. The journey was long and took several days as we were about, we stayed in a hotel in down-town Vancouver and experienced television for the first time. We also did some shopping, and I had an accordion bought for me as well as a real wool suit in salmon pink. On the way back we took a detour to Kamloops to look at horses and visited several ranches that were advertising them for sale. Our father was insistent on getting thoroughbred horses too which were extra expensive. We finally purchased a mare in foal and a young stallion, but we never acquired a saddle, so any riding had to be bare-back. I loved those animals and it made me feel that we were on a real ranch. I even got a cowboy hat to go with my chequered shirt and jeans. However, I never learned to ride the horses properly in the end.

I remember once incident which was rather unfortunate and upset our holiday. We were on the way back along the 800-mile journey from Vancouver, which took several days, when we came to a crossroad at Quesnel. There was no traffic and my father failed to stop at the sign at a crossroad and was caught by the police. We waited, wide eyed and I was most likely whimpering while our mother tried to keep us calm. It was a Saturday. The end result was that we had to stay for an extra two nights in Quesnel in order for our father to attend court where he was fined but allowed to continue driving.

I might mention here too that we went barefoot all summer which must have saved a lot on shoes. The soles of our feet became toughened as we were always encouraged or coaxed to run in the freshly mown and very rocky fields or on the gravel tracks and road. The joy of running barefoot on soft grass with the occasional deliberate step into fresh cowpats was great fun with the lovely squishy feeling. It wasn't so much fun if we stepped on a dried one full of beetles though.

Figure 14: Diana barefoot on the raft at river crossing

I learned to work with the cattle, how to herd them, call them and watch out for them. We had a pedigree bull called 'Blink Bonnie Lad' who was a lovely gentle animal, only dangerous when the cows were in season. There is a photo of me when I was about thirteen, climbing up to sit on his back, probably after a lot of persuasion. Grooming him was a good experience, especially if I found a lump containing a warble-fly larva which we could treat with a powder and remove. Calving season was most enjoyable unless there was a difficult birth and the vet had to be called. I loved the calves and adopted one which I named 'Little One' who had to be fed by us with a special formula, and I loved the feeling of her soft mouth tugging at my fingers as I spooned the formula in with my hand. I took plenty of photos of her with my new Box Brownie camera.

Figure 15: Hereford Bull - Blink Bonnie Lad

Tragedies happened with the animals, and I witnessed one cow which had fallen through the ice being rescued with the tractor and ropes. I wrote a letter to my grandfather in 1956 when I was aged ten explaining how we rescued a calf that had fallen down the well.

'One of our calves fell in the well and daddy ran back to the house to get us. Paul and Freida had to stay home, daddy got the ropes and chains, and we went down to the well we tied the rope around his neck and tied one end to a tree. We took an iron bar and put it in the middle of the rope and twisted it around and mummy held the bar. Daddy put his shoulder under the rope and tried to lift up the rope. Jon and I had to hold his front legs out. The calf made a low grunting sound and at last we got him out. About in the middle of the struggling I went behind a tree and sulked. We had a job to keep the cows away.'

Another cow was found dead, so I saw her being bulldozed into a pit with a stream of maggots coming out of her belly. If any of the animals were to be killed, I would run away into the forest as far as I could, so I didn't have to hear the shot, but that usually failed, especially when our horse Old Boy was put down. It was one of my saddest moments.

I learned a lot growing up on that farm. There was always so such to do like helping with fencing, stapling barbed wire, checking the line for breakages, feeding the animals, driving the tractor pulling a trailer, and by the time I was thirteen, a 3-Ton truck as well as the family van, eventually getting a driving license when I was sixteen. I took my test in January when we were experiencing 'black-ice' after a thaw and refreeze of the water on the road. We often had a warm spell called a 'chinook' for a few days at the end of December or beginning of January and then the real winter cold would set in. When I passed my test, I was only allowed to drive within a 50-mile radius until the driving tester came to Smithers from Prince George which was only a couple of times a year. Luckily, I passed that test too, both a written one and a practical one with our 'panel' van.

I learned about the farm equipment and how to deal with some of the little things to do with the tractor engine like checking the oil, decanting diesel from the big tank with a pipe and filling the tractor tank and greasing all the joints of the various implements. It might seem strange, but I loved the smell of diesel and grease which is often recalled when I go into a workshop or garage.

We were taught to swim in the river where our father had placed boulders to create a safe area and as the water was mainly meltwater from the glaciers in the mountains, it was extremely cold, even at the height of summer. However, we did learn and when we went for picnics at one of the local lakes, Round Lake, Tyhee Lake near Telkwa or Lake Kathleen near Smithers we could enjoy warmer water. There was an incident in our river eddy when some walkers passed by as we were learning to swim. I was puzzled as to why they were laughing at us. We had been given blown up condoms to use as floats, a fact I found out later, as well as the fact they were old fashioned ones made from an animal's bladder. This memory produced a poem:

Not Able to Laugh

At the bottom of the valley
by the bend in the river
where the gravel gives way to silt,
a woman tends her lettuce plants.

Nearby, a naked man is teaching
his three naked children to swim
in the ice-cold glacial melt of a river-pool
formed by a ring of granite boulders.

The children cling to their balloons-
their pink, inflated condoms,
nervously giggling from the cold,
paddling vigorously for warmth,

shivering to the laughter of a passer-by
amused at seeing three water-babies
clutching so frantically to their phallic floats,
and not understanding the joke.

06/04/2000

On the flat by the river next to our bathing area, the soil was very fertile, and mother had a vegetable garden that was always well stocked. She grew all sorts of vegetables such as carrots, cabbage, lettuce, runner beans and peas. The peas were always delicious, and we I always enjoyed helping her to shell them into a colander. We often helped her there if we weren't working on the farm. I, being the daughter of a Norwegian man, was expected to do everything a man did, even to hammering nails into the boards for building our New House and being a woman, was expected to help in the house as well. Mum, however, often took pity on me and let me off and I can remember falling asleep at the table after a long day and she just let me carry on sleeping.

Figure 16: Father, Jon, Diana, Paul, Helper

11- WHEN VISITORS CAME

My mother's brother Andrew came to stay with us a couple of times when he left college and helped on the farm and in the bush. We were all excited to see him and were sad when he left. Unfortunately, a few years later my mother received a telegram to say he had been killed in a plane crash. He had been flying his own light aircraft and nosedived into the airfield at North Weald just after take-off. Later we learned there were doubts about his mental state. He left a wife and two small children. My mother was, of course, devastated but once again, as my father couldn't stand crying, she wasn't allowed to, and she did her utmost to keep us children from seeing her tears. It was a sad time for her and for us.

My grandfather and Auntie Marjorie also came to stay with us twice during our time on the farm, once at the Old House and once at the New House. We were always so excited to see them, particularly as they were grandparents bearing gifts such as a large plastic red kite. It gave us a huge amount of fun until it got stuck at the top of one of the many tall trees that surrounded our property.

Over the years, prior to their visit, parcels from England arrived for every birthday and Christmas and my mother spent a lot of time in her letters thanking them and making suggestions as to what was the best gift for us. The parcels from England were always a delight to us, and Christmas was a special time.

Most of my collection of belongings arrived by post for my birthday or for Christmas. When I received a beautiful writing case from my Auntie Dorothy, I could write my thank you letters. Having always used a wooden nib pen it was wonderful to use a proper fountain pen and together with some aqua marine ink, I could write on real water-marked paper. How I loved the smell of that ink and the feel of the pen scratching on the paper. For some reason, I cherished the gifts from that particular aunt and still have the little needle holder she sent together with a pin cushion and a Knitting Nancy. She even sent me a very fashionable pleated skirt with twinset. I always hoped to emulate her with her style of writing which was, to me, perfectly formed and always so very straight across the page. However, I never did manage to. Sometimes I can't even read my own writing.

It wasn't until I returned to England that I met my grandfather's sisters or any of my cousins. This meant that the only relations we ever saw were my grandfather, my step-grandmother and my mother's brother, Andrew. Uncle Andrew also came bearing gifts. It seems to me that presents are important in keeping the memory of someone alive and those that I added to my collection always tell a story. Uncle Andrew with his handsome features and his dark hair who came to spend time with us in the depths of a Canadian winter, made an impression on me and I know my mother was happy having him to stay.

He did find the driving a bit difficult when it came to the icy roads because I remember him coming back from a trip to Telkwa having spun the car through 360 degrees. This incident seemed to amuse my father quite a lot but spinning the wheels, even with chains on, was a constant problem during those winters. Walking was quite perilous as we slipped and slid backwards on our way up the that steep the hill to the house.

My uncle did manage to make a few friends while staying with us as, so we didn't always see a lot of him. To me he represented the world outside of our valley and I always wanted to know about England. To this day I still have a small leather handbag and a charm bracelet with London icons like Tower Bridge and Eros in Piccadilly Circus.

Sometimes we had visitors to stay over the Christmas period and they were usually Norwegian. They were far from home, so it was an opportunity for them to have Christmas with a family, even if it wasn't their own. With the house decorated and the Norwegian element added, it was always a magical time. Our mother had two sets of decorated wooden plates with Norwegian folk songs painted on them, and these were displayed, along with a woven table runner. This meant that although I never learned the language, at least I could sing the traditional songs from the plates. One was about an old lady who walked with a staff and the depiction of the little bent woman with her black hair in a bun was what I imagined my Norwegian grandmother looked like. I don't recall having seen a photo of that grandmother while I was a child, but I did meet her later, even if it was only once.

As we got older, I would go with my brothers to find our own tree in the forest, cut it down and drag it back home. Some of the lower branches would be cut off and used to decorate the room over the doorways or above the windows. Our father had drilled a hole into a moose horn which made a good base for the tree and we would then decorate the tree with a few bought baubles, but mostly we would use items we made at school. My first decoration was a cardboard Santa in a paper sleigh. We also made paper chains and one of our dolls would be made into the fairy for the top. Most of our presents were practical items like new pyjamas, knitted jumpers, mittens, scarves but we always had a stocking as well. To us it was wonderful to find a tangerine wrapped in silver foil as oranges were a special treat. There would also be several small items in the socks from Father Christmas. He was Santa Clause too, with my Canadian friends at school. I don't ever remember receiving a lump of coal, though that was always the threat.

12 - THE GREAT OUTDOORS

I learned to ski the winter I turned six using plain wooden skis with leather bindings that fitted over our ordinary over-boots. Later we obtained better cross-country skis and proper ski-boots with proper bindings. These had a spring that fitted around the heel to hold the foot in place but still gave freedom to have the heel loose. Later still we progressed to cross-country skis with just a fixing at the toe and lighter ski boots. There were plenty of hills to use and we were rarely short of snow. Eventually when I was about fifteen, we went further afield, and I took part in a giant slalom race on Hudson Bay Mountain. The only way up was by tractor for part of the climb and then we had to ski to the top of the run. It was arranged by the Norwegian Ski club, and I came third and won a trophy. The ski-lift was put in a few years later. It was quite hair-raising as we were above the tree line and above the clouds to start and then zig-zagged through the trees. It was a bit difficult to see once I was in the cloud and I just managed to avoid having my skis dip into the well around one of the trees.

We were taught cross-country skiing and it was not until many years later, when I went to Switzerland, that I used down-hill skis. It was hard work sometimes but good for my fitness. I learned how to put the correct wax on for the different snow conditions and spent a lot of time on the slopes between our house and our neighbour's place. Our father had some sealskin covers to put under his skis and I tried them out a few times. The fur would act as a grip on the slippery surface so you could walk up the hills almost like using snowshoes. I never tried to ski-jump. Just coping with the bumps and the steep hills was enough for me. We would go for long trips taking a packed lunch and thermos flask of tea with us. I grew to love the sound of the skis shushing along the tracks and the click of the ski poles as we slid along. Our father was a good skier, as many Norwegians were, so we learned to ski the 'Telemark' method, a technique that combines elements of Alpine and Nordic skiing, which is named after the Telemark region of Norway, where the discipline originated.

I became quite proficient at it but once I left Canada, I was not able to continue with the sport. I believe it put me in good stead for the cross country running and eventual marathons that I completed later in life. When my marathon days were over, I took up Nordic walking which is much like skiing but without the skis. When there was a full moon and if the conditions were good, we would go out around the fields and enjoy some night skiing and we nearly always went for a ski trip on Christmas morning to let our mother get on with the preparations for dinner.

Figure 17: Setting off for a skiing trip

We had two very scary adventures while taking to the slopes. Our father decided one day that it would be a good idea to take my brother and me up the mountain and we skied to a point above the glacier when the weather turned, and we found ourselves in a blizzard.

We were more than lucky to get back down and no doubt our mother was most upset when she found out what had happened. I was fifteen when that happened and had been invited to go skiing with some friends in Smithers that weekend. You can imagine how upset I was when my father decided that he would take Jon and me instead as I would probably get into trouble with my friends, especially the boys.

The other time was when we followed our father across the frozen river, where some moose had crossed, and then proceeded to ski up a logging road into the forest towards a lake called *Coffin Lake*. I was about fourteen on that trip. Somehow, we got lost but continued to follow another track which seemed to go down and down for miles and miles until it became dark, and we could hardly see where we were going. It started to snow heavily and there was complete silence except for the sound of our skis and the click of our ski-sticks. At one point our father fell over a fallen log but recovered and coaxed us on and on. I was crying by now, and Jon was trying to be brave. My heels had been rubbed raw, the blisters having burst, and were extremely painful, but we had to keep going. The temperature had dropped to well below zero. Eventually we arrived at the railroad where we saw a house with lights in the window and surprisingly there was a woman outside with a lantern taking in her frozen washing. She got us into the warm and soaked the socks off my feet which had become stuck with ooze and blood. The pain of my feet thawing out was excruciating. She gave us some hot chocolate and we were able to telephone for a taxi. This was an experience I will never forget and nor would my mother who must have been sick with worry.

Figure 18: Beaver Lodge evidence Coffin Lake

We lived in hunting and fishing country, so there were quite a few occasions when I went along with my father and brothers. I did find myself, rather reluctantly, firing a rifle. I was scared of course. My father showed me how to hold the 303 rifles, which was used for killing moose, and how to line the sight up. I was then cajoled into pulling the trigger. He made me aim for a tree on the opposite side of the river, so I felt the reaction of the butt rebounding against my shoulder but never got to see if I had hit anything.

Saying this reminded me of one time when my mother was tending to her garden down by the river and someone from the opposite side fired a shot at her. At least she was convinced they did and came running home in quite a panic. We often had hunters around and there were always stories and gossip about how the hunters came up from the U.S. of A in order to 'git themselves a grizzly baarr' and tales of how they shot each other by mistake. Perhaps they didn't wear the essential red shirt to distinguish themselves from game.

Figure 19: Hiking to Coffin Lake

However, that was the only time I actually pulled the trigger and hunting was not really my idea of a hike, and hiking was something we often did. Up in the bush there were some trap-line trails made by the local First Nations People and no doubt early trappers. Some were still in use.

We would follow those trails for miles through the bush, passing leach filled ponds, climbing over or crawling under fallen trees, stepping through boggy areas with tufts of wild grass giving way underfoot. The trails continued through occasional clearings and over moss-covered patches with the earthy, frog smells of the forest. I was shocked one day when we thought we were in a quite remote and wild area to come across a discarded coca cola bottle.

It was my first experience of seeing detritus left by another human being in the pristine wilderness. We did come across the occasional forgotten trap or small abandoned hut, but that to me was only natural. To see a piece of abandoned scrap, even as a youth, annoyed me greatly.

Icon

High up here in the timberland,
along the trail of the trapper's line
by the clearing where the moose stands
knee-deep in a leach-filled bog,
where giant ferns hide the moss-bed
of frightened fawns and the air smells
of cranberries, decaying leaves and spruce -

Up here where I sit on this mountain ledge
looking down at the fertile valley
where the fast river, in full flow,
has cut deep and waterfalls tumble
into the canyon where salmon rise
to jump and flap upstream to the creek,
the fishhook or the bear's paw -

Here, beneath these Cathedral Trees,
the giant Redwoods, red of wood,
where branches turned to trees
balancing on branches turned to trees
from their mother root, centuries old,
reach sky-ward like tapered columns,
needled tips piercing a hanging mist -

Down here, on this pebbled beach,
where the Pacific strikes the coast
where otters cavort and seals slink
and crabs scurry around the rocks
beneath the path of haggling geese
arrowing across the morning skies
and where whales spout in the sound -

I found a Coca-Cola bottle. 19/04/02

Years later, when I was in correspondence with one of my First Nations' neighbours, he told me that his father had died while out attending to one of his trap-lines near a place called Houston, which was further up-river from where we lived. Somehow, I was glad to hear that he had still been carrying on the tradition of the North-western Interior peoples.

The Bulkley River was one of the best rivers for salmon fishing. Particularly the Steelhead and of course there were rules and regulations about fishing. Living just by the river meant that we were able to catch the odd one and we often had fishermen passing by. While we lived there it was rare to see a speed boat come upriver, especially when the river was running full and was bringing everything down with it, such as branches, whole trees with their roots showing, carcasses of drowned animals, cows or moose. But at quieter times we would see a boat with some fishermen pressing against the flow. We had many creeks where the salmon came to spawn and then we were left with the familiar sight of the dead and dying salmon which had made it to the creeks. The sight of those floundering salmon is quite horrific. They turn into the most grotesque creatures, but they have a fascinating life cycle.

Naturally with the salmon runs we had to watch out for the bears, and they could often be seen in the distance if we went to the edge of the plateau and looked down on the river flat. Where there were fall crops of oats waiting for harvest, we might see one moving through it or at least see evidence once they had rolled around and slept in it.

I never did turn into a fisherman. I loved the forest, the river and the mountains but was not one for dealing with the hunting-fishing aspect of living there. I preferred to use my 'Brownie' camera.

One Wrong Foot

The river, frozen over now,
flows fast beneath a rough
mountainous range of ice,
for January is the coldest month.

A man is making his way across.
He taps a tentative stick, testing,
seeking out a route to the sawmill.
His children follow in his exact footsteps.

A moose has crossed before them.
Her tracks trail out of the wilderness
past the timber shack by the frozen creek,
over the ice to the land of willow-bush.

The children stop to peer down a hole
chopped in the river's solid surface
hoping for a fleeting glimpse of fish,
a silver flash, but they are called away.

They'll work at the mill, stack lumber,
heave slabs onto the fire, roll logs.
Later, tired, they'll eat bread with jam
then climb into bunkbeds to listen for wolves.

18/05/00

VER OPEN February 2001 - Joint Winner
- Anthology 'Moods of Water'

– Adjudicator John Mole

13- SIBLING TIME

Babies became a busy occupation for my mother while we lived at the farm which, for some reason, had never been given a name that I can remember. Perhaps it was because all our post was collected from the post office in Telkwa from box 101 and we didn't have the usual rural box on a post at the end of the road. Those little 'houses' on posts were a very Canadian feature.

Eventually I was to become big sister to another four siblings born in the local hospital in Smithers. First there was Paul, two years after Jon, followed two years later by Freda, then Margaret and lastly William who is 13 years younger than me. Mother did have a still birth but once again there wasn't much fuss made, at least, not in front of us children. I became a little mother to the youngest ones and learned all about looking after babies, particularly as I spent a lot of time babysitting. It was always a delightful experience when mother came home from hospital after a week with a new baby for us all to coo over. Perhaps I was also glad to have her back as a lot of things happened in the household which lacked her touch such as having to eat re-fried porridge which I hated and my responsibility for making jacket potatoes which exploded in the oven. Little things like that could be quite irksome. Occasionally we would have some home help while she was away but as I got older, it was thought that I could cope and there was no need of extra help.

One of my younger sisters suffered from eczema as a baby and it was suggested that we gave her goat milk. That meant that we had not only a couple of nanny goats but also a billy goat. They were quite interesting animals to have and they got up to some amazing antics. First of all, they liked to chew the leather tack that we had hanging up in the porch and then they decided to jump through the kitchen window and caused havoc. The billy seemed to always stink, as mum would say - 'to high heaven' and my father would often tussle with him. I didn't like it when he took a hammer and knocked the poor billy as though giving him a head-butt, though I was assured that it didn't do the animal any harm and I was told that their heads were meant for butting. Toughness was a theme in my life. I was told that I should be as tough as or tougher than my brothers and as tough as a Norwegian. Perhaps there was something in that I did try to excel in everything I did, but there were times when it would have been more fun if I didn't have to always be stretching myself, to relax and just have fun like my friends at school. Perhaps I just envied them without knowing that they too might have been having tough times.

To be tough, us children found ourselves eating ants to prove we could, run barefoot through the stubble to prove 'mind over matter,' swim in the coldest of rivers without shivering to prove it could be done. It did prove true in that I can, even today, walk into a cold sea without too much fuss and I know I can eat ants if I was starving. As to my feet, they did toughen up as we went barefoot all summer. I still go barefoot at home and I can avoid flinching if I 'tough it out' over gravel. Perhaps some good came from it after all.

I did find it difficult to come to terms with the killing of animals though. Especially when I knew that a sack full of kittens were drowned in one of the ponds just over the hill from the house. I just loved kittens and to imagine them mewing as they struggled to breathe, always gave me a sad feeling as well as one of anger at having to put up with life on a farm. We had to be tough and being on the farm was not all kittens and roses. I was not even spared the butchering of a cow, which put me off drinking milk for weeks afterwards. Having experienced that butchering, I was quite miffed that I wasn't allowed to watch when a cow was having a caesarean section done by a proper vet, perhaps because the vet thought it wasn't something for a child to watch.

I had of course been used to helping with cows giving birth when my father had put his whole arm up the cow's vagina to turn a calf around. I had seen so much so why couldn't I watch the vet?

Barefoot in the Stubble

With feet left bare, what joy
to feel the dust of powdered soil,
the mush of fresh green dung
soft between the toes.

All summer without shoes,
except for going to town.
All summer hardening our soles
for winter's boots.

Yet you made us run
barefoot through that stubble,
tears stinging down our dusty faces,
wishing it would rain.

Why? For some thrill
witnessing our discomfort?
To prove some patriarchal point?
To toughen us up?

Yes, I can run barefoot through the stubble,
walk on hot sand without flinching,
creep over the gravel with no shoes,
but I can't thank you for the memories I have.

Back to the goats. I didn't like drinking the milk as it always seemed to smell of goats. It must have been good for my little sister as she thrived and was a strong 'bonny baby.' She was good at entertaining us by doing things like getting into the bathtub with her pretty floral dress still on. The babies always had a special baby bath which I believe was made from an early hard plastic material. The rest of us, while living at the Old House, would take turns using a galvanized bathtub set on the kitchen floor in front of the stove. After my parents had had their baths, I, being the eldest, was able to have my bath next and so on down the ages. The babies of course had their own. Getting the bath filled and heated was quite difficult as we only had the stove to heat the water on. In the winter, when it was difficult to get water to the house because of the snow and ice, we would go out and collect the snow in buckets to be melted down for our baths. Even the youngest sibling was sent out with a saucepan, so we all played our part. My mother was always wielding a camera and we had a lot of fun, once dressed up properly for the cold, as she clicked away. More 'snaps' to send to our grandparents. We all ended up with lovely rosy cheeks.

Figure 20: Collecting Snow - Freda, Paul, Jon and Diana

I always had my hair long and mostly in braids or plaits I would have to wash it in a bowl and rinse it with water poured from a jug. I then towel-dried it as best I could. In the summer I would go outside and run around letting the wind do the drying. My hair remained long as I was never allowed to cut it. My mother' hair had to be kept long and she always had it in a bun. I expect there would have been objections if she had tried to cut hers too. I loved using ribbons though. It seems I was allowed to have them. I always had big bows at the bottom of my braids and ribbons were always on my wish list for presents. Sometimes I would be sent velvet ones and ones that were in a plaid design.

As I grew older, I would put my hair up into a braided ponytail and try different styles like French braids, but only when my father was not around. The long braid with the ribbon at the end became my trademark and is how some of my classmates remembered me when we had a forty-year reunion. There is a picture of me running around a track in a relay race with my one braid following behind me.

Being able to drive the family car was a bonus once I reached sixteen. Prior to that, as the fall fair at Smithers was always held at a difficult time on the farm, the only way my brother and I could go to it was by hitch hiking. The one time I remember doing it, we had walked about three miles when luckily a neighbour came by and offered us a lift. We had a great time getting there, bouncing around in the back of his pick-up in the open air and clinging on. There were few rules and no seat belts then. At the fair we met a few friends but were careful with the money we had been given. We even managed to have some money left. Perhaps we had been treated, but I don't remember, and nor do I remember how we got home.

When I finally had the full use of the car, I could drive into Smithers with my brothers to the drive-in cinema. I was even able to take some friends with us on the Dollar Night. We were allowed to pack as many people as possible in the car on this special night for just one dollar for all of us. It was one of the few times I felt grown-up and a member of a gang with my classmates. It was also at a time when I had a bit of freedom when my father was away in the mental hospital at Essondale. I will explain this in more detail later.

There were some things that were drummed into me which I guess could be classed as beneficial. First there was the business of alcohol. As far as I can remember, my father never drank alcohol and the only time that a bottle of beer appeared was when there were too many wasps. A couple of bottles were bought to see if the wasps would climb in and drown. This meant that I also never tasted alcohol until much later in life. I don't even remember my mother having a glass of wine or a beer either.

As to cigarettes, I became so frightened of them that I was even afraid to pick up a cigarette in case I caught cancer. I was told a tale about how some old Norwegian men would chew tobacco and spit it at the back of the stove. It was down to his wife to scrape it off and it was through this contact with the tobacco that she caught cancer.

Consequently, I have never even had a puff of a cigarette to this day and I must say I'm glad of it.

14- FAUNA AND OTHER CREATURES

I have mentioned that we were living in bear country. We often saw evidence that a large bear had been around when we found patches in the field where one had been rolling around, flattening the crop. Evidence was also seen in the spoor left which was full of berry seeds. I was afraid and would sing my way along the road to let any wildlife know I was there. One day when I was in my second year at school, aged eight, I was dawdling home alone when I noticed a black form in the top of a cottonwood tree located behind our neighbour's house. I decided that I would do a good deed and tell them about it as there had always been a fear that cougars were about, and they were considered extremely dangerous. The neighbour's son came out with his gun and I scurried ahead, ducking under a barbed wire fence that was at the edge of their property and got well past their house. I looked back and saw someone take aim. I heard the shot ring out and saw a baby bear tumble out of the tree. I was so upset when I realized what I had done that I never forgave myself and to this day the memory is still vivid.

Bears often came near to the house and we were entertained by a mother bear with her two cubs that came right outside our windows which were large and acted like a picture frame to the outside world. We watched as they clawed and sniffed and tested a cow's hide that was stretched across a wood frame for tanning. They were there for ages until someone brought our little dog, Turi, to watch with us. She got overly excited and made great fuss barking and jumping up against the window. The mother bear immediately stood up to her full height, sniffed the air, then thinking better of it, turned and lumbered off, her little cubs following closely behind.

Another bear incident happened to me when I was in charge of taking a bucket of food to our neighbour's dog when they were on holiday. Their house was about a mile away and the road went down through a poplar grove to the river flat, passing through forest to a cattle grid. Once over the grid the road followed along a ridge to the neighbour's house. It was just before I reached the cattle grid that I saw a bear cub by the side of the road. I had been told never to come between a mother bear and her cub, so I just dropped the bucket of dog biscuits and ran back up the hill and home. I refused to go back so my mother had to go and finish the job for me by which time the little bear had disappeared. We decided that he was probably an abandoned two-year-old as the mother would have had a new cub to raise and it was usual for them to be left to fend for themselves at that age.

My encounter with a lynx in the middle of the forest while out running is described in my poem 'Forest Run.' It was one of those moments when my senses were heightened with a fear that is difficult to explain. I remember feeling as though I belonged to nature and the wilderness. The original title of the poem was 'On Crown Land near Telkwa' but I decided to change it to be less specific.

Forest Run

Fall and a sprinkling of snow.
Jogging along a logging track
through the darkening timber
of lodge-pole pine and Sitka spruce
balancing on the edge of ruts
frozen ridges of churned mud
fleeing a teenage angst
desiring aloneness
respite from filial demands
paternal clutches
I came upon a clearing.
By a pile of sawn logs
ageing under the heavy light of snow-cloud
I stopped to listen to the silence,
to feel the stillness,
to breathe the freedom.
Then, out from the camouflaging background
of the woodpile, like an apparition,
a lynx appeared, tufted ears alert
still as a sphinx.
We observed each other for an eon
as something passed between us
some recognition
something other than fear
some affinity with our shared wilderness.
We turned away in unison.
She, to slink back into the forest,
me, hair bristling down my neck,
to run for home.

July 2001
The Result is what you see today (Poems about Running)
Published by smith/doorstop books – The Poetry Business- ISBN-
978-1-912196-81-4 2918 – Diana Moen Pritchard – October 2019

I mentioned wolves earlier, too. One winter when we were fairly well snowed-in at the Old House and our father was over in the bush, it was getting late and nearly dark. My brother Jon looked out the window and called out 'Daddy's here!' and promptly opened the door before our mother could stop him. There was a scream, and the door was slammed shut. A timber wolf was standing outside in the swirling snow watching the house. I have no difficulty remembering that incident. There had been a lot of snow and high winds with blizzard conditions at the time and a pack of timber wolves had been spotted by our father a few days before, so I suppose it was no surprise the reaction my mother had.

Often, over the years, we would hear the wolves howl and the coyotes bark. We even heard cougars making strange sounds. Wolves were the ones that always made a shiver go up my spine. It was a long, piercing howl, primeval, part of the wilderness, but it was the coyotes that would keep us awake. The sound of their barking and howling often sounded more like dogs squabbling and seemed to go on and on all night. There were a few years when I heard no wolves, presumably they had been culled to near extinction, but the winter before I left Canada, I heard them once again. Wolves howling and the sound of the train's warning as it snaked along the track on the other side of the river pulling its mile-long set of boxcars were all sounds of my childhood.

The train with its cowcatcher at the front in case a moose or cow was on the line was a familiar sight as it passed by several times a week. When we heard the train, we would run outside and try to count all the boxcars. It was another form of entertainment for us isolated children. From our farm perched on the plateau above the river flat, we had a good view of the train which ran along the opposite side of the river that flowed in a northwards direction towards Telkwa. We had a wonderful view when we moved to the New House and could see far up the valley. In the fall, the colours of the poplar and birch trees were vibrant against the greenness of the spruce and pine.

When we first moved to the Old House, we had a cocker spaniel given to us called Tuffy. We also had a few cats, one we called Ginger who, being a male, often left us at the beginning of the summer and we wondered where he had gone, but he always came back again in the fall. It was a thrill to see him return, usually more battered and scratched with a chunk taken out of his ear. The first one who spotted him would call out 'Gingy's Back!' but, of course, there came a time when he never returned. Some of his progeny lived on and multiplied and at one time we had about ten cats all the same colour, a pale fawn. One of them disappeared for nearly three weeks and was found by mother when she was checking on firewood. He had got caught in a rat trap and was very weak from lack of water and food. He survived but lost his foot. Not long after this, the cats caught a disease and one by one we would find them dead by the front door. It was as though they were coming for help, but being outdoor cats, we could do nothing for them. It was always sad for us children when our pets died. The cats, though, seemed to really have nine lives.

Looking from our New House towards the hills on the other side of the river, I spotted a white object on what looked like a cliff. When my father got his telescope out, we discovered it was a mountain goat. He got extremely excited then and decided to go across the river and see if he could shoot it. This he did and we ended up with mountain goat for the freezer and a lovely white hide. We took the hide to Mary George, our First Nation neighbour, and she cured and created a lovely rug trimmed with little triangles of red felt. It became a favourite rug of mine.

Porcupines were another animal that foraged about in the woodland and one day our Norwegian elkhound, Turi came home with porcupine quills in his nose and around his mouth. That was unforgettable. The only way they could be taken out was by using tweezers and pulling them straight out but for that we had to call a vet. I think my father tried to pull some out first but poor Turi was too distressed. It must have been extremely painful. I think the vet brought some anaesthetic with him. It made me realize just how dangerous those quills could be with their barbs like fishhooks. They couldn't just be pulled out the way they went in. Turi made a good recovery and I'm sure he kept his distance if another porcupine appeared. He was a rather inquisitive dog.

Turi came to us as a puppy. He was a pedigree and I remember the excitement of going to the railway station to collect him. He had travelled across Canada by train and my imagination ran wild thinking of that tiny puppy having to spend such a long time in a cage on a train. He was a lovely animal and gave our family a huge amount of pleasure. I always feel sad when I think of his demise. Our family were all leaving, and he was to be a wedding present to some friends of ours but before then he had made friends with some people on a construction site down on the river flat where they were extracting gravel. Apparently, he fell asleep by one of the big movers and he got run over as the driver didn't realize he was there.

The summer we moved to the farm and the Old House; we had an invasion of grasshoppers. They were giant greenish brown insects that ate through my mother's vegetable patch at great speed, gorging themselves on the meadow and planted grass crops. They were frightening and set me off screaming. It was such a horrible feeling having them drop down my neck as I went through the door and, together with the sound of them munching, made me very squeamish. I had to walk home from the bus stop trying to avoid them as well as the large, persistent mosquitos and the masses of blackflies. The blackflies were devils and always bit me behind my ears leaving a crust of blood.

For some reason, I didn't feel them bite. I would often try to just run through the clouds of flies or mosquitoes and hope to leave them well behind me. The grasshoppers were something else and they even chewed through the mosquito net that was protecting my baby brother in his pram.

Just before I left Canada, in June 1963, we had a plague of Tent Caterpillars. Those creatures were far worse than the grasshopper invasions we had had over several summers previously. They covered everything with tent-like webs, ate all the leaves off the poplar trees leaving them look like skeletons much like a winter scene. When they got squashed on the highway the road not only had a horrible smell, but the surface became very greasy and dangerous. Even the trains had to go carefully and were delayed as there were patches of caterpillar grease on the tracks. So, we experienced not only good and bad with pets, delight and fear with wildlife, we also had the mosquitos and other insect pests. Mosquitos were of course a yearly problem and because we lived with wildlife all around and areas of marshland, stagnant ponds, and other places for mosquitos to thrive in, we had a constant battle. By the end of the summer, we seemed to have built up some immunity to the mosquito bites and I would often let them fill themselves up on purpose so I could slap them dead in a cruel sort of way. I was getting my own back.

I have several more poems about my wildlife encounters, a selection may be found in my anthology titled 'The River's Bend.'

15- OUR HOMES

As I mentioned earlier, we had no electricity at the Old House, and we had to rely on a coal-oil lamp with a wick and glass cover or a lamp that had twin gauze mantles and a pump that hung from the ceiling. All my homework was done by those lamps until we moved to the New House and the electricity was put in. An incident happened with one lamp which could have been disastrous for us children. I was babysitting and our parents were out on the farm somewhere, it was getting darker and darker.

My brother Jon said he wanted to light the ceiling lamp. I was against the idea, but he insisted, so he lit a match and held it up to the mantle, probably climbing onto the table to do so. Within seconds, flames shot up towards the ceiling and I yelled for him to get out with the other children. He seemed to freeze and wasn't prepared to listen to his big sister. However, I managed to persuade him, perhaps because I yelled so rarely. My screams should have been heard a mile away. While he led Freda and Paul out, I grabbed a towel, as we had been taught, and managed to smother the flames. I really don't know how I did it, to this day. I shudder when I think about what could have happened. At that time, I was about ten, Jon was eight, Paul six and Freda nearly three.

The house was made of logs and had a shingle roof so if it had caught light, we would have lost everything. The chimney featured at Christmas time too, when we would write a letter to Santa and put it in the flu behind the stove then dash outside to watch it fly out of the chimney in the blackening smoke. It was a mystery to us how Santa could possibly read them when they had been so scorched. There again there was a danger and we had one or two chimney fires that had us all running out of the house to wait while the fire was dealt with.

When we moved temporarily to the sawmill site and camp by the railroad, we often saw the 'speeder' or 'pump trolley' pass by us along the track. It was used by the railway workers who inspected and did repairs to the tracks. It moved along at a reasonable speed with one of the workers pumping a lever. The first ones we saw were the hand-pump version but sometimes a motorized one would pass and could go quite fast. That was another bit of entertainment for us as we told our younger siblings to watch the 'speeder-go-by' being a new word to our vocabulary. The men would wave back to us too which was fun for us while we were living so cut off and remote.

It was here, too, that for several seasons, some eagles built a nest right near the sawmill. The eagle used to follow the tractor as it pulled logs down from the bush and would pick up bits of bark to build the nest. Unfortunately, one summer some hunters came and shot at the nest, so one of them was either killed or they just flew away to nest somewhere else. I was terribly upset to think that someone could be so thoughtless.

I have mentioned the New House several times. From the earliest days when we moved into the old log house, my father had plans to build a new house positioned at the top of the hill with views up the valley towards Hudson's Bay Mountain. It was to be made of concrete with picture windows, a basement containing a water tank, and a couple of floors with a flat roof. Not at all like the normal Canadian houses. I think, in hindsight, he may have been influenced by the concrete bunkers the Germans built during the war, solid, secure, and long-lasting. He spent a lot of time planning and making drawings, but funding was a problem. He had to earn enough in the bush and at the sawmill as well as from selling cattle. Money was tight and although us children didn't really understand the financial problems, we often found ourselves with our mother in town visiting the accountant. Later, in her letters to her father, I found out just how much of a struggle she had to put food on the table.

Figure 21: Cats with Mountain View

Eventually my father started to build the concrete house and I would spend a lot of time as I grew older, together with my brothers, hammering in nails and pulling out nails as the shuttering was formed and iron rods inserted before being filled with cement mixed with gravel from our land on the river flat. Contractors came in to pour the concrete, but we also made a lot of it ourselves using a cement mixer attached to the tractor.

Figure 22: Living in Basement with cow on roof

It took several years for the house to be built and for all the pipes and wiring to be put in as well as having the walls plastered and the double-glazed picture windows fitted on the first level. We moved in on 1st December 1957 when I had just turned eleven, but it was far from being finished. Initially we all had to live in the basement until the spring when we could have some rooms ready on the first floor. It was a bit chaotic. When we finally moved upstairs, all the children except for me had bunk beds in the basement. I was given my own room at the back with one of the picture windows facing a poplar grove. My brothers and sisters might have been jealous that I was the only one to be given her own room, however for me, it came at a price.

We still had to use an outside toilet as the new internal ones were not fitted until much later. In winter, the trail to the outbuilding with its two seats of different sizes and newspaper squares for toilet paper, was like an ice run. There was no way we could just 'nip to the loo' without pulling on warm clothes and putting boots on.

When our English grandparents came for their second visit, which was now at the New House, us children were full of joy. Auntie Marjorie arranged flowers and I was impressed with her display of wild flora in an old, galvanized tub. Our Norwegian grandparents, unfortunately, were never able to visit us. They occasionally sent us Norwegian story books based on the American series of the Katzenjammer Kids called 'Knoll og Tott' which fascinated me. The books didn't help me learn Norwegian, though, as I had no interest in learning that language. I hated having to listen to the drone and monotone of the conversations my father had with any Norwegian friends, helpers or workers who came to visit or occasionally live with us. They were always very friendly, and I particularly liked Gunnar Berge who spent a lot of time with us, returning to Norway to see relatives and coming back to continue to earn money to send home. He also played the violin which we enjoyed listening to. One year he brought his son Nils back from Norway with him, but he only stayed for a short while.

The New House could have been a good, modern house, but sadly it was never finished. We even have photos of cows lying lazily chewing their cud on the flat roof of the first floor. Mother did her best to decorate and bought our first refrigerator which she had painted brick red and she also painted a set of chairs and the table in glossy black. It was in this house that we acquired our first gramophone to play *Little White Duck* and my first record, Limbo *Rock* by Chubby Checker. And then there was the joy of using a telephone, even though it was a party line. I would spend a lot of time talking to one of my friends who lived at the Agricultural Experimental Station and I would play my accordion to her over it. Having that telephone was to me an amazing and welcome development, but we still didn't have a television set like all my friends in Town. The only time I saw a TV was when we went on the holiday to Vancouver when we had not long moved into the new house.

I think our lives were fairly typical of rural families in the area post WW2 and we felt very much like 'mid-century' pioneers, especially when we went over to the other side of the river to clear land that had been purchased at Hubert. Great windrows were formed of all the trees and shrubs which were later burned. Wild fruit was in abundance in those windrows too, raspberries, black berries and huckleberries thrived, and we would pick buckets full. There was another berry which we loved to pick called *Saskatoons*. They were a delicious dark berry similar to a blueberry, very fleshy and sweet. We often went on blueberry picking forays, tiny sweet blue berries on low shrubs. There was even a hill on the highway called Blueberry Hill. Once when we lived by the sawmill, a First Nation's grandmother would walk past us from having trekked several miles along the railway track to pick blueberries and what a treat it was when she gave us some from her bucket. My mother would offer her a cup of tea and she would rest a while before continuing on towards Walcott where she lived. We loved to watch out for her as she ambled along the line towards us.

We knew the times of the trains and could also hear them coming from many miles away, so we always felt safe. We invariably practiced balancing on the rails and would compete to see who could go the furthest before falling off. A few one cent coins became misshapen on those tracks too, much to our amusement, especially if we thought our parents didn't know.
Our father often had ideas of moving us even further into the wilderness and he was particularly interested in land on the edge of Babine Lake, the longest natural lake in British Columbia. He went so far as to take my brother Jon and me for a four-day boat trip around it, a journey of about 200 miles. There was an American family living by the lake at one end who had moved

there to be safe from the threat of war with Russia and I met their daughter Mary Lou who was my age. I found it fascinating to meet someone with such a strange American accent. It was late summer too and there were eagles circling and loons calling on the lake as well as salmon in the creeks. However, it wasn't where I wanted to be, and I was glad to get home. That boat trip around Babine Lake was not a great one for me. I didn't like having to sleep under the upturned boat with my father while my brother slept outside. It was a week of having to put up with him using my body for his satisfaction.

Had we moved there, we would have been too far away from any town or village and we would have had to be home schooled. We would definitely have been mid-century pioneers then, with land to clear and a house with barns to build. It would have been a terrible interruption to my life as I had formed good friendships at high-school and had my sports. I also had plans that I would go to university in Vancouver to follow a career in teaching. I even I belonged to the Future Teachers' Club at the Smithers High School.

16 - A Turning Point

I was very much an introvert during my childhood. I wouldn't say 'boo to a goose' as I once heard someone say about me and kept myself to myself a lot. I enjoyed the company of friends who were loud and seemed to be at the centre of things. Sport kept me safe. Running became my therapy in later life and being alone never bothered me. I could dream of another life away from the restrictions imposed on me. I could never cut my hair or even be allowed as much as a little 'kiss-curl' on my forehead without being told off by my father. Almost from an infant in my cot, I had secrets to keep. As I became a teenager, I was told I must not speak to boys and that if I fell in love with one of them, it would show on my face and in my eyes and I would be in trouble. I found it difficult to look anyone in the eye and I grew to hate myself, my face, and my reflection in the mirror. ` My life was a lie from my cradle until I was released from the dominance of my father when, in 1963 he was finally sent to prison and I was spirited off to England.

(I later found out from my mother that when I was in my cot the midwife caught my father lying right inside it beside me and suggested to my mother that she 'watch him.' At the time I guess she didn't understand why, but that was most likely when he took an unnatural interest in me as he made me do things right up until his final arrest when I was sixteen.)

For many years my mind had blocked out the bad and the 'you must not tell anyone,' 'the police will come and take me away,' 'the family will break up,' 'many Norwegian girls become their father's wives so there is nothing wrong but it must be a secret.' Occasionally over the years I have had 'flashbacks,' particularly when I learn of some other child having to go through the same difficulty as I had. I was often told by my father that my mother was no good, lazy, cold and from such a privileged background that she could never live up to Norwegian standards. He tried to convince me that I was special, but it only made me feel more inferior.

There was never a woman who worked so hard as my mother. She had a very productive garden, she kept all of us children fed, well dressed and clean despite us all having to use a metal bathtub in front of the stove, taking turns with water heated on the stove. There was always a bowl of warm water on the kitchen table in the morning when we needed to get ready for school and for us to wash our hands before dinner. Most of the time our father was away working then coming home and expecting his food to be on the table. Even so, he always told me she was no good, silly and unintelligent. And so I endured, keeping myself to myself for the sake of my siblings and my mother as I did not wish the family to break up, and I thought I was protecting my sisters from the same fate. How many times I bit myself in frustration, tore the buttons off my pyjamas, and tried to avoid my father's attention. I remember particularly the incident with the pyjamas because I had ripped the material in my exasperation and when my mother saw the tear against the buttons, she was angry because she would have to make the repair and I couldn't tell her why I had done it. I had only torn them after my father was out of sight as I was afraid that he would be angry if he found out. Self-punishment became ingrained. I sometimes drew blood when I bit between my thumb and forefinger and I would sometimes scratch my forehead.

I hated having to sit on his shoulders when I was still an infant and not too heavy. He would put my dress over his head as a joke. He thought it was fun to bounce me about and I would squirm to try to get away from his prying fingers.

If he was out with me and my brothers, he would often get them to go off to do something so he could get me on his own. He even wanted to watch me when I squatted to urinate so I would hold on as long as I could bear in order to have my privacy. He always seemed to find an excuse to get me to sit on his lap as well and I hated that too, especially when he pushed himself against me and I knew that even though he was fully clothed, he was having an erection.

From an early age I remember having to wash my father's back when he was taking a bath. I just hated doing it. I don't remember when I first became aware that there was more to it than just having fun scrubbing his back or when my innocence was lost to the reality of the situation, but I really grew to detest his bath days in that tin bath with all the grey soapsuds turned to scum. As I write this, certain things that happened seem to come back to me which I must have blocked out for most of my life.

He continued to educate me. He told me that if a man was walking a bit funny it was because another man had been putting his c... in his bottom. There was a family term for the private parts of boys and girls which might be from Norwegian, but I am unable to write down or say those words to this day. He also told me that what he was doing to me with his fingers was gently breaking my thing like a skin that covered my hole so that when I grew up it was already open and wouldn't hurt me when my husband did it. I didn't know then, of course that he was trying to break my hymen. I would squirm and ask him to stop but I was usually trapped. He might have placed me on the table or if we were outside in the bush, it would be on some moss. It could be anywhere where he thought it was safe. I would always look away and cover my face and imagine I was somewhere else. I think I thought if my face was covered it wasn't actually happening to me. I would also hold my knees together a tight as possible and he would just force them apart. Sometimes he gave up and I could feel he was upset with me. He was also extremely careful to get rid of any evidence.

It was always 'this is a secret,' 'mummy cannot satisfy me,' 'it's normal and it's not wrong.' Then one day, when I was about fourteen, I heard my parents having sex and I was so sickened by the fact that he could say my mother was no good when it was obvious that she was. I did everything I could to avoid being alone with him.

I had learned to keep quiet and I never ever allowed myself to have eye contact with anyone just in case they saw through the deceit. If anyone asked how I was, I was always 'fine' with a smile. I think I eventually lost the smile too because I remember later when I was happy about something, I was told: 'Smile. It may never happen.'

It was all kept a secret from my mother, of course, who did her best to keep us all healthy and happy and the farm animals fed and watered. When a welfare officer came to see us once, she complimented my mother on how well she was bringing up us children despite the difficulties. The years went by and I kept the secret fearing the repercussions if I ever told anyone.

He continually justified what he was doing as well and threatened me in all sorts of ways if I didn't comply. I just had to pretend nothing was happening and if I was a bit sore and my mother asked why, I must have found an explanation of some sort. I had to be extremely careful that I didn't say the wrong thing, so it was best to just keep quiet. There was no one I could talk to about it either and he didn't like me having friends. I did have friends, but I didn't let him know that I did. In other words, I had to keep secrets from him too.

My father became increasingly paranoid, thinking that the forestry commission and the big saw-mill businesses were trying to force him out. He would lie around a lot doing almost nothing but talk about new projects and inventions and plans to take the whole family to live in the wild beyond Babine Lake. When he lay on the couch, I would try to be somewhere else in case he got me to lie beside him. I just hated having to scratch his back. I don't think I ever had a proper unconditional cuddle from him.

In February 1962 he eventually had a complete breakdown and threatened to kill the family by driving us into a canyon or kill himself. My mother, who had spent a lot of time trying to cope and keep him calm, decided to go to see the doctor. She arranged for him to come out to see my father but first, on his advice, she took us children with her to stay with some friends in town. She then waited while the doctor went out to the farm accompanied by the RCMP. - Royal Canadian Mounted Police. There was a standoff and a chase through the snow and into the bush while he was brandishing a rifle. Eventually they caught up with him, he was arrested and taken into custody.

He was committed to the mental hospital in Essondale, in southern British Columbia where he stayed for three months getting treatment. He was diagnosed with paranoid schizophrenia. This was in June 1962 when I was fifteen. When he came out, he found some work doing night shifts in Burns Lake, meaning he was away for the week only returning home on weekends. Things seemed to be okay during the fall of that year.

While he had been away, I had had a bit of freedom and was able to stay in town with friends and even found a boyfriend. I excelled at sport and enjoyed playing basketball as part of a team. In the years prior to that my father would never have let me join any team. He objected to my doing any extracurricular activities or going to dances. The high school 'sock-hops' were great fun and I also took part in a school play dressed in a Hawaiian costume.

I had some excellent teachers and although my grades were not brilliant, I enjoyed all my lessons. I joined the 'Future Teachers

Club' and sometimes acted as a monitor in one of the more junior classes

The summer was for track meets, both interschool and local. I joined friends in Smithers for picnics. In the fall and winter, we had toboggan parties, skied with friends, went to dances and generally life was peaceful and fun. Mother continued to run the farm and sort out the sawmill while she was winding things down.

I was invited to the graduation ball for the year above me by Erik Peters and I remember the lovely green dress my mother bought me from a little boutique near Smithers Airport. Erik sent me a beautiful orchid corsage which I later kept in the fridge and eventually tried to dry. My father was not told about the ball or that I had a boyfriend. I dreamt of going to Vancouver to university and also had dreams of training for the 1968 Olympics. When my father was able to come home, things didn't get better for me or the family, finally coming to a head in June 1963. It happened when I had moved into the new bedroom. The door had no lock. I could hear the handle being twisted and the door creak open. I pretended to be asleep and even tried to make a snoring sound when he entered the room. He had been let out of the mental hospital and had made promises that he would never do things to me again. He had been cured. He was standing beside the bed and hovering over me. I kept my eyes shut tight and hardly dared to breathe. I could hear my heart thumping. He stopped for a short while and then left. He must have thought better of it. I moved the wardrobe against the door the next night hoping that he wouldn't try again but if he did, he would get the message. It was as I had feared. I heard the sound of someone creeping towards the door. I was being extra alert. I felt panic and my heart was thumping again. The latch was once again being rattled and door was being pushed. I held my breath listening for the wardrobe to move, which it did but only slightly.

He tried to shove against it a couple of times but gave up. He must have realized I had blocked it. I was really scared then because I thought about how angry he would be with me the next day. The morning came and nothing was mentioned. A few days later I went for a run through the bush and he must have been following me. He suddenly appeared out of the woods, and I stood my ground. He said he just wanted to talk and wouldn't hurt me, but I avoided him and managed to persuade him to leave me alone. I remember feeling quite sick. He went off begging me not to say anything.

I plucked up the courage to talk to my mother, having come to trust her during my brief time of freedom. Up until then I think she didn't realize how far my father had gone with me. Maybe she was shocked or maybe she had suspected for some time. However, she decided to speak to the doctor again who told her that I absolutely needed protection and I should be sent to stay with friends while she sorted things out. My father was then arrested, and I had to go to the hospital to be examined. I was also questioned at the police station and made a statement. A very friendly Mountie guided me into a room with a big desk and gave me some paper and a pen. He asked me to write down all the incidences of being sexually molested, so I wrote and wrote and wrote. Eventually he returned and said 'That's enough now little girl. You don't have to write anything more.' I had not finished, and I was almost reluctant to put my pen down, but it was such a relief to have been able to tell someone.

My father was charged with attempted incest and imprisoned. For several months before this, my mother had been discussing the possibility of me going to England for a holiday and to stay with my grandparents. She arranged for me and my brother to have a passport and for my grandparents to send the money for the fare. As far as I know, my grandparents were not told anything other than that I would be going to stay with them for the summer. Quite when they were told the real reason I do not know as nothing was ever mentioned to me. I think they probably thought it best not to discuss it particularly as it wasn't a great subject to be bringing up with a grandchild. However, it was decided that I and my brother would both go to England to live and the rest of the family would follow. Our mother had to organize the sale of the farm and attend Court in Prince Rupert to get her divorce. Luckily, I didn't have to face the court as well, though for some weeks I had an overwhelming fear that I would. Another reason that it was a prudent move for me to leave at that time was that the upcoming court case would most likely have reached the local newspapers and it could have made life difficult for me having to face my friends. I found out many years later that quite a few people had found out about it.

My brother Paul flew to join us in England a bit later and my mother took the three younger children across Canada by train and then by ship back to England, once she had obtained her divorce.

I had to say my sad, sad, good-byes to all my friends and to Erik of course. I had really wished to stay in order to take my final year at school so I could graduate. My headmaster was very hopeful that I would, as my prospects were fairly good, even though my grades were a bit lacking due to my home problems. However, it would have been difficult to live in the area if the court case got into the press so it really was prudent for me to move away and although my father had an injunction against him, he wouldn't be incarcerated forever and I needed to be free of him. My friends held a party by Lake Kathleen for me with a 'wiener-roast' and music. It was summer, the weather was lovely and the beautiful lake with the majestic Hudson Bay Mountain and the wildlife were seared into my memory.

I never saw my father again. A new chapter to my life was about to start back in the place of my birth, England.

Treasured possession

White gold with diamond chips.
That first love ring lies cossetted
deposited in its velvet-lined box
with silver lock and pearlized lid.

Those were days of sock-hops, basketball,
drug stores with soda fountains,
shy glances and giggling in the toilets
between *Phys-ed* and *Home-ec* lessons.

His courier sister passed me the note -
Invitation to the '63 Graduation Ball.
I was in grade eleven then as the crush
moved on to the dance at the high-school hall.

At the Wayside Boutique on Highway 16,
just past the drive-in, mum bought the dress -
light green chiffon and lace to wear with nylons
and my first high-heeled shoes.

The orchid corsage, pale purple and cream,
arrived by taxi in a see-through carton.
I kept it for weeks in the fridge
then later dried in a book, long gone.

I left for Europe that summer.
Friends held a party by the lake.
A *weiner* roast with hot dogs,
marshmallows and bottles of coke.

He wrote letters, sent flowers, and visited once
when he toured the world with his rucksack.
Then Interflora stopped delivering.
I never sent the ring back.

6.11.94 Dedicated to Erik Jorgen Peters,

17 - CHANGE

July 1963 was the month of drastic change for me and for my family. Jon and I boarded our first ever aircraft at Smithers' Airport and flew from Smithers to Vancouver where we stayed the night with Arthur and Jean Soper, cousins of our grandfather William Soper. They were most helpful to us and took us to see Stanley Park, later giving us a memorable chicken dinner. Next day they brought us to Vancouver Airport, and we flew to London Heathrow. As this was my first big international flight, I was intrigued with all the tiny items like sugar and salt packages and folding spoons and kept them as souvenirs for a long time afterwards. We were given a meal of chicken in tiny dishes. Grandpa was there to meet us with his big Jaguar car and drove us through London to the farm in Old Harlow, Essex. I had never seen so many houses. There seemed to be nothing but buildings all the way. We arrived very tired of course and were treated to yet another chicken dinner. I was given the bedroom at the side of the house that overlooked the farmyard so I could see everything that was on in the busy yard. It also overlooked the dog kennels with two Labradors and the stable block with two horses.

The rest of the summer was filled with so many activities and I think Auntie Marjorie really worried about entertaining us. We went for a week to Norway to visit our Norwegian grandparents, an adventure in itself. We got to know uncle Torolf and Auntie Inga and her husband, Jens.

*Figure 23:
With my Norwegian
grandparents and Jon
- My pale green ball dress*

We were taken to the Royal Agricultural Show near Birmingham where we also met one of grandfather's sisters, Auntie Mable and her husband Uncle Walter, however the highlight of that trip was seeing the Queen who was attending the show too. It was at this show that I had my first encounter with English colloquialism. I was contemplating the turnstile and wasn't sure how to get through being afraid of pushing. Suddenly someone called out 'Hurry up ducks' to me and I felt so very foolish. I had never been called a duck before.

Next, I found myself going for a sports coaching week at Lilleshall Hall in Newport, Shropshire where I did some athletic training. In the strength tests I had a stronger push-pull than the top athletes of the day, Anne Packer and Mary Rand, who would have been my contemporaries. Unfortunately, I didn't have the correct or latest techniques required to compete at a high level without a lot of coaching and commitment. However, I joined the Harlow athletic club and did a bit of training on their track and went to one or two local meets where I specialized in the hurdles.

The summer ended after we had a short holiday by the seaside at Cromer with Bunty and Eddy Fisher in their caravan with their two children. Bunty was employed by my grandparents to look after the horses. She tried in vain to teach me to ride a bicycle on one that was far too big for me. I think it was an old one belonging to a farm worker and was more suitable for a man anyway. I had never been to the seaside except for when I was a baby, and we were lucky with the weather as I don't remember it raining. It was also my first experience of living in a caravan.

One special trip that I took with my grandfather required an exceptionally early start. He had a market gardening business at the farm in Old Harlow which was started when his son Andrew was still alive. It was called W. J. Soper & Son, later changed to W. J. Soper Limited. This meant that he sold his vegetable produce in

London and had his own stalls at Covent Garden, Spitalfields and Borough Markets. Lorries would bring produce to market and return vegetables and fruit that he didn't grow, such as Canadian Delicious apples, to sell to greengrocers, among others, in and around Harlow. He asked me to accompany him to Covent Garden in the early hours of the morning when he went to check on the stall and liaise with his buyer there. This was while Covent Garden was still a fruit, vegetable and flower market. It was an interesting experience for me, and I was glad I had the opportunity to see the market before it lost its Old London feel with its barrow boys and bustling buyers and sellers. It all seemed to me to be so very 'English and Old World.' Ever since that visit, I have always had an affinity with London. Somehow, I felt connected with its history and London was to become part of my life later on.

As my grandfather had a housekeeper as well as a gardener, farm workers and other staff running his business, he had a very structured life. I learned to use the knife and fork the English way, not that my mother hadn't already taught me, but this was real to me. Before dinner he always had a glass of sherry and I was allowed to have a glass too. There was always a nicely laid breakfast with either a boiled egg with a silver spoon or poached egg on toast, marmalade, pats of butter, some cereal. I had been used to porridge which I hated or just cereal, eggs being more for a main meal.

I had what I considered the privilege of sitting in the tall Wingback chair in the living room, which was covered in pale green velvet. That chair became special to me and became 'my chair.' It was the one I perched on when I watched my first television coverage of a tennis match taking place in Wimbledon. My grandfather and Auntie Marjorie played tennis themselves on the lawn in front of the house and often had guests to play, all dressed in white, followed by 'afternoon tea.' It was in black and white and I remember my grandfather being particularly keen on watching

Margaret Smith and Billie Jean Moffitt. I had, of course, never had anything to do with tennis as I hadn't lived in town and no-one, I knew had a tennis court. It was a new experience for me, and it was also wonderful to actually watch 'TV' as we never had one on our farm in Canada.

I felt that I was now really learning the English way of life, but I did miss my friends from school and although everything was exciting and new, I was quite homesick for Canada. I wrote long letters on airmail paper to Erik, and he sent beautiful letters back. I was overwhelmingly sad having had to leave him and I had no idea if I would ever see him again. I was heartbroken. Luckily, I had so many things to keep me busy in this new life I was getting to terms with that it helped me cope. I was glad, though, that I was free from my father and knew that he couldn't get in touch with me in England by order of the Canadian courts. Even so, there was always a slight nagging fear that he might find a way of following me.

18 - TAMED

WILD CANADIAN TO ENGLISH BOARDING SCHOOL

Now it was time for me to get on with my schooling. Letters were sent back and forth between my mother and my grandparents to come to an agreement as to what schools my brother and I should go to. Eventually it was decided that Jon would go to Mark Hall School, which was local, the entrance being opposite the farm. I was to go to an 'all-girls' school as a boarder in the cathedral city of Peterborough, Northamptonshire, where the head teacher was a friend and university colleague of Auntie Marjorie. Perhaps it was thought best as I would be safely away and also because I needed to adjust to a whole new curriculum, after all, my history lessons and geography lessons were mostly about Canada and not Britain and I needed to get British qualifications. The school was called Westwood House and was located on the banks of the River Nene.

What a change to my life that was. I had to be kitted out with a uniform which comprised of a red and green striped blazer with pleated green skirt, a straw-boater hat for summer and a green felt hat for winter, stout brogue shoes, long green all-weather jacket, scarf, tie, green bloomers for gym, stockings, green and white striped summer dress, grey suit with grey felt hat and another pair of stout shoes for going to church on Sundays. I also needed a hockey stick, long knee-length socks and boots. For the summer I had to have a tennis racket, white collared shirt and white shorts as well as a swimming costume and cap.

The swimming pool was outdoors and unheated with the leaves from the nearby oak and elm trees floating in it. I had been used to cold swimming but somehow that pool felt extra cold. I also felt the cold and shivered more in the damp British winter than I ever did in the coldest Canadian winter for some reason, perhaps that was the difference between the dry-cold climate I had been used to and the fact I had always dressed for the outdoors better. What a contrast all this was to my casual Canadian attire. I was really taking a plunge into a different culture from the co-educational schooling I had been brought up in.

My principle, Joyce Bowis, was kind yet firm with me and I kept in touch with her over the years until her death at the age of 100. She tamed the wild Canadian girl very sensitively and I am always grateful for that.

So it was that I learned more of the 'English way.' My colleagues would persuade me into their circle and make me recite *'the grahs grows green around the cahstle'* without the rolling of my 'r's.' I tried and tried but my 'r's always rolled as they still do today. In Canada I now have an English accent but in England there is confusion. Is my accent from Devon or Cornwall? I am often asked but no one has ever thought my accent was American, I'm glad to say.

I coped with the curriculum fairly well but had to go into different class age groups as it was a bit different to my Canadian one, particularly with maths. I had never touched on *sine* or *cosine*, and I had to get used to Pounds, Shillings and Pence instead of the decimal currency of Canada of Dollars and Cents. I wanted to do chemistry which wasn't offered by the school, so I had to go to a boy's grammar school once a week for lessons there. I learned to sew with a treadle sewing machine and made a white apron for cookery and a baby dress with smocking. I excelled at athletics and played hockey and tennis, rather badly I might add, but won the trophy for sports that year too. I also had dancing lessons and learned to waltz foxtrot with a lovely teacher whose deaf friend played the piano for us. It was all far more elegant than the wild dancing I had experienced in Canada with the stomping barn dances, square dances and other folk dances from Norwegian, Scottish and Irish backgrounds.

I made several good friends at the school and eventually shared a room with one friend later on. I shared my dormitory with three other girls, and this was another experience that was alien to me.

I continued to miss my Canadian friends, particularly Erik and we kept writing letters to each other. He even sent me flowers by Interflora for my birthday much to my delight and I think some of the girls were envious. Some of the other girls had boyfriends which they could see when they went home for half term or for Christmas, so I was envious of them.

My grandfather sent a crate of Canadian Delicious apples for me on one occasion, but I had to put it in the 'tuck' room and could only get access to them once a day. Having a Canadian connection made me feel proud when I shared some of the apples with my classmates.

One November day while at the school, 22nd November 1963 to be precise, some friends came running to me in my dorm to say that President Kennedy had been assassinated, an incident that was engraved on most people's memory of the time. I did have to explain that I was from Canada and not the USA though. I listened to the news on a little battery radio I kept under my pillow so I could listen to the latest Beatles music. Later on, I listened to the first British pirate radio station, Radio Caroline, which started broadcasting from a ship off the Essex coast in 1964.

I was not able to go home to Old Harlow every half term, unfortunately, so I went for one holiday to stay with my mother's cousin Peter Davies and his wife Jane who lived on a farm out on the Fens. They had a couple of children, one of whom, Tony, nearly drowned in one of the dykes. I came to really like East Anglia, particularly as I had to go from Old Harlow to Peterborough by train through Ely with its big Cathedral, via March, a long journey over flat countryside, quite different to the mountainous Canadian terrain I had been used to. Somehow the countryside with its wide, open skies attracted me. One time, coming back on the train to Harlow, I got off at Sawbridgeworth by mistake and my poor grandfather must have been very worried sick as he was waiting for me at Old Harlow station. I eventually got a message to him, I do not know how, and he came to collect me from Sawbridgeworth. I always thought it a coincidence though, as I was actually born in Sawbridgeworth in a nursing home in Bell Street. It was as though I was meant to return to the place of my birth. The home was eventually turned into a pub and restaurant.

I have a lot of memories from my English school education, and I believe the discipline was good for me. I didn't leave with many O Levels due to the fact I was only there for one year, but it stood me in good stead for my future writing. My typing skills started in Smithers High School, but they weren't continued in Westwood House, as the subject was not taught there. I also developed my love of poetry as my English teacher was besotted with Keats and *Ode to Autumn*. She also organized a trip to the theatre in London to see Shakespeare's Hamlet with Peter O'Toole as Hamlet. I was impressed with the acting as I had never been to any kind of play or live theatre. Peter O'Toole and Omar Shariff were both to be in the film 'Lawrence of Arabia' a couple of years later and I must say that I swooned over both of them.

So that year passed and in July 1964 I left the school and returned to Old Harlow. By then my mother had established herself and the other children in a house at Glover's Lane, Hastingwood, Harlow. I left my grandparents' house and moved there too. There were not many bedrooms, so I used what was called a 'box' room while living there. The house was a typical Essex village cottage with shiplap timber cladding painted white. It was certainly a house unlike any of the ones we had lived in in Canada.

Next on the list was what I should do as a career. I took some aptitude tests to see what would suit me. I was an outdoors person so one suggestion was to join the police force. I didn't like that idea but after lots of discussion it was decided that I should improve my typing skills so I enrolled in a 'fast-track' intensive course, two years crammed into one year, in shorthand, typing, secretarial and office procedures. The course was at Marlborough Gate Secretarial College, 62 Bayswater Road, London, right next to Hyde Park. I was to become a secretary!

Figure 24: Me in red suit at Marlborough Gate College

19- I Move to London

During the summer of 1964, I continued with my athletics at Harlow Sport Centre and there I met Piero. I had become friendly with his brother Lakis first as he was also into athletics, and he introduced me. I found Piero, who was eight years older than me, to be quite charming. He had dark curly hair and deep brown eyes with a ready smile and a permanent tan which I envied, having quite a pale complexion myself. It was an exciting time. I fell in love.

I was almost over the fact that I wouldn't be seeing Erik again. I was sad that our correspondence had to cease but I kept the letters from him. He was left-handed and had the most wonderful handwriting. I even kept a ring he had given me when he visited me in England on his travels through Europe. He said it was for me to keep and that it wasn't an engagement ring. I often wondered afterwards whether he did mean that or not.

However, I had now met Piero. People told me how well we seemed to match and that we looked good together. Perhaps it was because he was dark haired, and I was blonde and also maybe it was because we looked happy. I didn't see him often as he was living in London and only visited his mother in Harlow on occasion. Once I was going to college in London, we would

 meet up more frequently and when my mother moved from Hastingwood to Kitchen Hall Farm, he would come to visit me there.

Figure 25: Kitchen Hall

I would travel to London from Hastingwood by bus from the bus stop at the Bull and Horseshoes Pub to Epping, then take the London Underground directly to Lancaster Gate in order to get to college. After making the journey for several months, I moved to London to share a room in the YWCA with a girlfriend I knew from Peterborough. The address was Helen Graham House, 57

Great Russell Street right opposite the entrance to the British Museum. So now I was to become a proper Londoner. I got to know the area well and enjoyed my time at the college where some of us students worked hard at upping our typing and shorthand speeds. It worked a bit like a spelling bee where some of us tended to compete to be the fastest, so we progressed through our certificates at speed. It was meant to be, of course, as we crammed the two-year course into one. I have certainly never regretted becoming proficient at touch-typing. I would go home to Harlow for weekends but eventually I started seeing a bit more of Piero, who, unbeknown to me, was married.

My friend Sheelagh from Canada came to London and I left the YWCA so we could share a bedsit together in Westbourne Grove, near Lancaster Gate tube station. It was in a terrace of town houses with bay windows. Our room was at ground level with the bay window. We had a little *Baby Belling* stove and we had to share a bathroom with others in the house. Eventually my friend left, and I then moved into a similar bedsit in a house with Piero which was owned and let by a Greek lady who lived with her son in the rooms above. I still had no idea he was married and even when we met up with some of his friends, nothing was mentioned.

It was during this time that I would sometimes meet Piero at his uncle's restaurant in Camden Town after work and before going home. I sometimes helped with waitressing and it was there that I found that I enjoyed eating Greek food. Piero had quite a few connections with the Greek Cypriot community there and he seemed to have cousins all over the place, most of them hard at work in the clothing industry. One of his uncles had a restaurant and another one had a photography business in Camden Town. Piero had connections with the casino community in Mayfair as well, having befriended a man call *Wilfred Hyde-White*, whom I later learned was an English character actor, known to gamble. We were invited as his guest to an evening at a London Casino and this was quite an experience for me. I had never been inside one and had no idea about the card games or betting chips. I had put on one of my mini dresses, had my hair up in a 60's style and wore little blue earrings. There was a spread of amazing food on a long table and I remember having salmon. It was when I went to the 'powder room' that I realized how out of place I was. There was someone sitting by the entrance taking coins and providing a towel and in front of some mirrors were plush fur covered stools. Sitting putting their powder and lipstick on were women dressed in long elegant dresses with real diamond jewels dangling from their ears. I have never felt so underdressed in my life with that cheap blue dress and plastic earrings. I was quite overwhelmed and upset as I had had no idea just what to expect. I was so glad when we left, and I have forever kept away from casinos. Piero no doubt enjoyed himself and at that point I had no idea of how gambling had taken over his life.

One evening I was to meet Piero at Mornington Crescent underground station and he was running late so I sat down on a bench on the platform keeping myself to myself. There was a lift because it was an exceptionally long way down to use the stairs. I found myself alone and the train passed through only stopping every other time. I tried to make myself small and insignificant, but I was approached by a man in a long black overcoat. He came right up to me, was breathing heavily and opened his coat to flash his private parts. I avoided looking at him as best I could and got up to leave the station by climbing up the stairs. I was afraid to summon the lift. However, I could hear a train coming so descended the stairs quickly again to find the platform empty and I jumped on the train to the next station. It was an experience that probably happens all the time on the underground, but I was quite angry with Piero for being so late and I felt so vulnerable. We were still in the early days of our relationship, so I guess I was forgiving.

I made a few good friends at Marlborough Gate College and we often met up at one of the pubs next to Hyde Park for a vodka and orange or glass of Blue Nun. I wasn't much into drinking, but it was a good atmosphere. One of my best friends was Edna from Iran whose father worked at the Iranian Embassy. Her parents had been friends with the Shah of Iran before he was deposed, and Edna had been to finishing school in Switzerland so spoke several languages. I was always amazed to see her write shorthand in English, write to her boyfriend in Persian, speak to her friend in French or German and then converse with me in perfect English. We also raced each other on the typewriter to increase our words per minute as well as seeing who could progress through the shorthand exercises the quickest. It was an excellent method of learning, cramming so much into so little time but it worked well for me.

When I finished my year and received my certificates, I started looking for a job in London. I went for one interview with Vicks VapoRub Company but didn't get offered the job. However, one day Piero and I were walking down Lower Regent Street on the way to The Mall when we passed British Columbia House. I didn't know that the individual Canadian provinces were represented in London apart from Canada House. Piero suggested I go in and ask if they had any job available with them. Now, I am not one to just go in and ask, but he persuaded me to and so I went in. I was told that 'in fact the receptionist was leaving' so I could apply for that job. I had an interview and was told that I would hear from them in a month's time.

We had planned a holiday to Greece with two friends, Mary and Graham who had known Piero for a long time, particularly Mary. Graham was a rugby player with the Upper Clapton Rugby Club. The trip was by train via Munich and south through Europe to Greece where we would be guests of a Greek dentist and his wife. Piero was a Dental engineer, and he was going to do some repair work for the dentist in exchange for us using his holiday home on the island of Hydra. It was a memorable holiday particularly as the dentist had two sons about the age of eight or nine who tried to get me to speak Greek.

The island of Hydra has no natural water for drinking, so it was delivered by tanker on a regular basis. It was dry and hot there and we spent a lot of time swimming in the beautiful clear water. It turned out that I was the only one not to get sun burn because I wore a light long-sleeved blouse all the time, even when I went in for a swim. I remember plastering my friends and Piero with yogurt which was supposed to help stop the pain and bring down the redness. A lesson was learned that holiday. I also enjoyed the lovely smells of dried herbs and lavender and the taste of the fish. It was the first time I had ever eaten octopus or a whole fish, eyes and all other than from a can of sardines. The weather was perfect and so was the sea. I fell in love with Greece.

Because at that time we had to pass through customs at every border as we went through Germany, Austria and other Eastern European countries I found it a fascinating journey. I had never seen guards with guns before and they seemed to be everywhere as we passed through the stations. I particularly remember Skopje where a child was trying to sell us items at the station where we stopped for water and seeing the farms still using the old methods of farming with hay stooks, donkeys and overladen carts. I was struck by the poverty and rural-ness.
The journey was long, and I spent most of my time observing the countryside, following the maps. Map reading was one of my

passions as I always wanted to know where I was in the world. My travelling companions, however, spent most of their time playing cards, and as I could find no interest in playing cards, I had plenty of time to indulge in viewing the world outside the window.

On returning to London, I received a message from B.C. House to say they would offer me the job, but I needed to telephone them so that Mr. Graham Gibson, assistant to the Agent General, Earl C. Westwood could hear my 'telephone' voice. I spoke briefly to him and he told me I was hired and could start the next week. I was grateful that my boyfriend had been so persuasive It was a wonderful position to be in. I was paid a Canadian salary which was a lot more than I would have received as a secretary anywhere else at that time. I learned much about London, the theatres, the hotels, bus routes and the London Underground because most of my duties, apart from arriving first to open the post, were to help travelling British Columbians find accommodation and give directions on how to get from A to B. One visitor who came, even took me to lunch. It was Harry Wearne whose sole aim was to see the gorillas at London Zoo. I mentioned him in an earlier chapter. I worked at BC House for two wonderful years, expanding my knowledge of London, enjoying the sights and sounds of the big city, improving my secretarial skills, meeting Canadians and generally feeling I was a Londoner.

My mother had arranged for me to have a holiday just before Christmas, which she paid for. I think she was hoping I would find a different boyfriend. Perhaps she worried about the cultural difference and also that Piero was eight years older than me. I went with the Youth Hostel Association to Kandersteg in Switzerland for a week and I have to say I had a fantastic time. The group I was with had not been before and I was experienced, though only with cross country skiing, not downhill so I found the bindings rather difficult. However, I didn't have to have many lessons so was out on the slopes nearly all day. The 'après ski' was wonderful with the wine and melted cheese on big chunks of bread. I even came down from the top of the mountain with some good skiers and the instructor while the others took the gondola down. We had to stay in a hotel for one night as our hostel had been double booked. This meant that I had an amazing bed with an eiderdown and a mattress that felt as though I was sleeping on a cloud. It was a memorable holiday with others my age and being back in the snow, delighted me. The holiday ended when I got back to the station in London and there was Piero to greet me. My mother's idea had failed.

In July of that year, 1966, I discovered that I was pregnant. I remember being incredibly nervous when I had to tell my mother. I don't remember her reaction, but I don't think she was overwhelmed with joy. It was not planned. The 'pill' was something very new and I had not started taking it yet. It was then that I found out that Piero was married. I was terribly upset, of course, but he promised he had left his wife before he met me and wasn't having anything to do with her anymore. He could get a divorce very quickly. His mother even asked me if I was sure I wanted to keep the baby, but I wouldn't even contemplate having an abortion. Perhaps she knew something more than I did about her son and I expect she also knew he was married but felt it wasn't her place to tell me. Besides, her English was limited. However, I guess I was in love and thought we would be fine with a baby to look forward to.

20 - BECOMING A COMMUTER

At the end of August 1965, I had moved back to Harlow with Piero to live with his mother and brother at The Glebelands. We commuted to London on the Greenline bus from Harlow to Epping and then took the underground. I changed at Tottenham Court Road and got out at Piccadilly Circus to take the short walk to B.C. House and Piero went to his work at Portland Street.

The journey was not particularly fun as this was before the underground carriages were improved and the floors were still made of wooden slats. Cigarette butts and ash filled the gaps, and I would often arrive at work with a blackened collar and stuffed up nose. As my tummy swelled and started to burst through the buttons of my winter coat, I found the journey quite uncomfortable.

During this time, I must say that I began to have a few problems with Piero. He would lose his temper and sometimes would punch me in the stomach and on one occasion he actually kicked me there. He may have been thinking that he didn't want to be a father, but he always apologized, and we made up.

I left my job at Christmas 1966 and Martin was born on 21st March 1967. I had moved back to live with my mother briefly at Kitchen Hall Farm and Piero came to stay. He was a heavy chain smoker, and our family didn't smoke so my mother had to have a fan installed in the en-suite to the bedroom we stayed in. Meanwhile it was arranged that Piero and I would move in permanently to the flat at The Glebelands. Elektra was moving back to London and Lakis had already moved out. Luckily, the council allowed her to transfer the flat to us.

I gave birth to Martin on my own in the Princess Alexandra Hospital, Harlow, as Piero said he had jobs to complete and was having job interviews. I felt very much alone, and I was determined to keep things to myself as my mother was too busy. Elektra was away at the time too. She had left London or gone back to Cyprus to be with her mother who was well into her 90s.

It was an exceedingly difficult time as I was three weeks overdue. It was decided that I should be induced. During the birth, my face swelled up on both sides of my neck and I was told I had surgical *emphysema* where air from my lungs escaped to form bubbles under my skin. I looked like a hamster but as my hair was long, I had it parted in the middle to hide the swelling which did eventually subside. Occasionally a student would come to see me and ask if they could feel my neck which squelched horribly. When touched the air moved and made a crackling sound, a bit like the popping of Rice Crispies. I was happy to let them as it was so unusual. I always wondered if the air out from my lungs and under the skin as I was breathing the gas and air in so deeply. Martin was whipped away to the Intensive Care Unit as he was jaundiced, and I had no idea whether I had a boy or a girl. A nurse had to go and find out for me and I couldn't get to see my baby for over twenty-four hours. She also asked me, when she returned to say I had a boy, whether the father was foreign. I wondered just what my baby looked like. I was getting desperate. My mother eventually came to see me accompanied by our family doctor and they saw to it that I could go into the unit and hold my baby for the first time. I was so relieved and overwhelmed to see him and hold him even though he was a bit yellow. Unfortunately, I had to breast feed him behind a screen in the unit. At that time, it was frowned upon to expose a baby to the outside world while feeding at the breast. During the hours that I was unable to see Martin, I had been put on morphine as I think the doctors thought I was in pain from the swelling, so I found myself hallucinating. I thought I could see Piero was coming towards me along the corridor, but he wasn't. The whole episode was both frightening and surreal. Piero did eventually arrive a couple of days after the birth with a gift, not of flowers or chocolates, but a pot plant.

Martin was, to me, a beautiful baby weighing 7 lbs. 4 oz. I wouldn't have been without him for the world. As he got older, I carried him on my hip as I had done with my baby brother William. I was so lucky to have had the experience of learning about babies with my younger siblings. With the help of *The Common-sense Book of Baby and Child Care* by American paediatrician, Benjamin Spock, I was launched into the career of bringing up a child.

While living at Kitchen Hall, I would walk down to the local shops at Potter Street, about half a mile along the edge of Harlow Common, pushing the pram. On one of these trips, I left the pram outside the bakery shop briefly as most of the other mothers did and suddenly someone came running in to say that a man had taken a baby out of a pram. I ran outside to find that Piero had arrived off the bus on his way to see me at Kitchen Hall. He had seen me go into the shop so picked Martin up. I was so relieved that it was him and not some stranger. At the time it was not thought a problem leaving the prams outside the small units, particularly as they were all glass fronted and you could get a good view of the square from inside. It did scare me to think what could have happened and I became a bit paranoid. It was also a bit upsetting that I hadn't expected Piero to turn up on that day. At the back of my mind, I always carried a fear that my father would suddenly turn up one day unannounced. That fear lived with me for many years, and it wasn't until my father died that I finally felt freed from that anxiety.

I continued to stay at Kitchen Hall for the first few weeks but eventually we moved back to council flat at the Stow. It was a rather cold place on the second floor of the block but very convenient for the shops and other facilities of the town. I could go for long walks along the cycle tracks and we were close the

Town Park. There was a playground below the block with a green area with trees which was very pleasant in the summer. The first winter there, though, was very cold and the walk to the shops was treacherous. I felt trapped for several weeks when Piero decided not to come home and stayed with relatives in London while the weather was bad. Occasionally I would take Martin to visit my mother and the rest of my family who were still living at home.

It was a struggle for us. We didn't have much money. Piero's wages didn't go far, and I didn't have a job. We had our family allowance for Martin. I did try to take on a job sewing plastic baby pants, but I found I didn't have the skill without an industrial machine. I also did a little bit of modelling for the art class at the local college, fully dressed I might add. I had a good friend with a daughter born at the same time as Martin. Her husband was an art teacher at the college.

I had to eke out our money. Luckily, I was given small weekly allowance by my grandfather from a family trust he had set up for his grandchildren to go towards funding their education. It was meant to tide us through until I could get a permanent job. Piero left for London early on his motorbike and got back extremely late most days. Lakis came back to Harlow to continue his studies at Harlow College and stayed with us which helped towards the rent and some of the household bills. We often had Cypriot visitors and Piero's relations to stay. It was a trying time for me as Piero tended to spend some, if not most of our money at the betting shop. He would watch the results on the TV on Saturday mornings and on one occasion he smashed the set in his frustration and anger. His brother always tried to calm him down and usually succeeded but I wasn't so successful. In hindsight of course, I should have realized that I was now stuck in a controlling relationship, but I didn't because I naively thought he would change, things would get better and we had a child.

Piero was a very charming person, loud, boisterous and the opposite of me who wanted to hide among the shadows.

There were times when I found it almost impossible to cope and I remember looking out of the window to the pram where I had left Martin briefly while I took the shopping in and having an overwhelming feeling of sadness. What was my little son's life going to be? How would it turn out for him? Perhaps I had a premonition of things to come.

I found a child minder eventually and found employment at the Key Glass Company in Edinburgh Way, initially starting as a temp but they offered me a permanent job. At least I could buy some groceries and pay for childcare while we tried to save.

I worked as a receptionist and did all sorts of office jobs such as making tea and coffee, filing, checking invoices and generally being a 'Girl Friday.' The days were long, and I was lucky to have such a good childminder. Martin was only about six months old when I was back working full time.

21 - RETURN TO CANADA

The summer and a very cold winter passed with things much the same until we decided that we would emigrate to Canada. Piero spent a lot of time in London, getting back late and there were often arguments. I found a couple of friends to visit so Martin had someone to play with. Disposable nappies were not on the scene yet, so I had to soak Martin's nappies in solution and used an old-fashioned tub washing machine with a wringer. My hair was long, and I once caught it in the ringer but luckily was able to yank it out hard enough to release the safety catch. When Piero was home, he still continued to go to the betting shop at the Stow and on Saturday mornings he would watch the races on television. I was glad his brother was there to help keep the peace.

Piero had still not got a divorce. One day I found a pawn ticket for a pearl necklace. He must have explained it away but looking back I am convinced it was one that belonged to his first wife. After all she was an heir to a French supermarket chain. I had already seen him pawn his watch and had also gone to the pawn shop to pay for an item of his mother's that had been left there. I still thought he would change as he said he loved me, and we had decided that by emigrating he would stop gambling and our lives would change for the better.

Piero applied for a visa to go to live and work in South Africa first, before settling on the idea of going to Canada but he told me that they were only accepting white people in at the time. Admittedly Piero did have dark curly hair and darkish skin. He found out that he wouldn't be able to get a visa to work in Canada either. If, however, we were married he would be able to qualify under my Canadian citizenship as I could sponsor him. The other obstacle was that he had to get a divorce first. Obviously now I had been told about his marriage, which he assured me was over when he met me, we married on the 13th January1968 and finally, in June 1968 with Martin only just over a year old, we managed to get through all the paperwork. Piero found a job to go to in Toronto as a dental engineer and with a gift of the fare from my grandfather, we set sail from Liverpool, retracing the steps my parents took in 1949. I was returning to Canada.

We said our goodbyes to my mother and younger brother at Kitchen Hall Farm. Mary and Graham as well as some of Piero's friends and cousins were there too, to wish us well.

Seasickness was an issue and I remember that Piero spent nearly the whole voyage in the cabin. I went to the doctor for a jab so I could cope with my little boy who enjoyed running around the ship to the delight of many passengers. I did have plenty of childminders on that trip. We arrived in Toronto and were met by Piero's employers who helped us find accommodation. We rented two rooms at the top of an old house which looked great from the outside but harboured an army of cockroaches. Not pleasant.

Figure 26: Martin, 15 months, sits for his passport photo

The house was owned by a Greek Cypriot woman who had a love of shoes and I remember she brought about a dozen pairs of various styles of Italian shoes and tried to persuade me to buy a pair. She was a flamboyant character, but I wasn't that pleased about the accommodation she was providing us. If I put the light on at night to tend to Martin, there would a scurrying sound as cockroaches scuttled into the various cracks and crannies of the room which had linoleum flooring. It reminded me so much of the grasshopper invasion of my childhood, especially if any of them fell from the ledges of the ceiling onto the bedding. Heating was also a problem, or rather too much heat. As we had the top floor all the heat rose from the rest of the house. We did have a sort of balcony out over the roof and I rigged up a playpen for Martin and because we had so little money, I bought a second-hand blanket, folded into four and whipped the edges with blanket stitch so Martin had a cover for his cot.

There was another couple living below us with a small child too, so we had company. Brenda was a tiny woman, and her husband was at least six and a half feet tall with a big build. When he held their little girl, she seemed to disappear in his hand.

He was a 'gentle giant' and worked as a builder. Brenda was also quite stubborn and one day she was driving me, Martin and her baby somewhere through the busy city traffic when we had to stop at the traffic lights. She was a bit slow at starting off and, as was the usual case if you didn't race off on the 'go' some agitated driver behind you would honk. That driver honked and Brenda sat through the light and I believe she may have sat through the second one too. She wasn't going to let anyone honk their horn at her. They were a lovely couple but of course they weren't from Cyprus, so we didn't really get to know them very well.

I eventually found a nursery school nearby run by an English woman. This meant I could at last look for work. Unfortunately, Martin wasn't there for long before I was informed that he was too boisterous for them as he wouldn't go to sleep in the afternoon when they were supposed to, and it disturbed the other children too much. The problem with finding a new childminder was eventually solved.

There was one occasion when Martin fell ill and had an extremely high temperature. I was on my own, Piero was probably at work, and I was desperate as I didn't know just what to do. I had no transport, so I wrapped him in a blanket and took him on the bus to the Children's Hospital in Toronto. The journey seemed to go on and on and I was extremely worried. As soon as I got to A&E, he was whipped out of my arms and given a tepid bath to cool him down. I learned a lesson then, but it was a very worrying time. The efficiency of the hospital was impressive as they gave me a plastic card similar to a credit card and it gave all the details necessary so if I had to take Martin to hospital again, they had all his information. At that time Canada was leading in the field of computer technology.

When I started looking for work, I was surprised to find that having had training as and English Secretary, my skills were in great demand and I found a job in July 1968 with a refrigeration and steel tank fabrication company, J. H. Locke and Sons, where I was employed as a receptionist, doing a bit of this and that, making tea and coffee, typing letters, arranging meetings and helping with advertising and checking time sheets for the salesmen. I was even asked if I minded climbing up onto one of the large steel tanks for a photo to put in an advertisement. I agreed, of course. A month later, in August 1968 I was offered a promotion to be the secretary and assistant to the chief accountant for the company. I worked on payroll, prepared statistical reports, and did general basic accounting. I made good progress there, checking the timesheets of the salesmen, doing up the wages, collecting and depositing money at the bank. For dealings at the bank, I had to sign a bond, and this was a position to add to my CV. It was a super job, and I was well paid, but I had to move on. A bigger salary was required so we could move to better accommodation.

We moved into an apartment in the Don Mills area of Toronto. I was relieved to leave the town house. We didn't have enough money to furnish the apartment properly so only had some basic items which were bought on hire purchase. Even though I was earning good money, Piero went back to gambling again, if he had ever stopped, so his wage packet rarely made it home.

Figure 27: Toronto - Piero with Martin

He found a group of Cypriot men who played cards so spent a lot of time with them, mostly away in one of their houses leaving me on my own with Martin. He would eat there often too, so the meals I cooked for the both of us were wasted. I rarely got out to meet people and wasn't able to have any friends. If I did ask if he minded if I went for a lunch with a colleague or a drink after work, he would refuse to babysit, and I became stuck at home.

I found it difficult to write to my mother, so I didn't contact her for many months as there was never a right time and I didn't wish to upset her. Eventually I had a visitor from England. He was the Company Secretary for my grandfather's business and was on holiday in Canada visiting his son. My mother had asked him to check in with me which he did and of course I told him everything was okay and that I would write to her soon. I felt bad about it, but I did as I always felt I had to do in those days and that was to smile and say 'I'm fine. Thank you' when I was aching inside to say that I wasn't.

We had many Cypriot visitors and went on picnics with that community to the lakes and parks in and around Toronto. My hopes that Piero would stop gambling were completely dashed. He soon started going to the racecourses on weekends and often played poker late into the night and early morning. He would lose an average of twenty to thirty dollars a week. In September of our first year in Canada, he went for a holiday on his own and lost over five hundred dollars on the horses. A lot of time was spent in the company of Cypriots and as I didn't speak the language, I felt superfluous. They tried to welcome me, and I tried to respond. I was often asked for help or guidance with things like 'what name should I call myself to fit in to Canada?' Michalis became Michael, Stavros became Steve and so on. One of the newest arrivals to Canada, who was a diligent worker on a production line for car seat covers, asked me why her boss had told her to slow down. I explained that it was probably that the other workers who couldn't keep up with her were complaining. Many of the Cypriots were very skilled at things like sewing and were used to 'grafting' but found it difficult to fit in unless they were with their own community. I had another go at trying to learn Greek but without success, particularly as I was always mocked by Piero for not pronouncing the words properly. Not long after I had met him and was first introduced to his mother, he had asked me to repeat one set of words over and over again to get it right. I then proudly said them to my future mother-in-law. It turned out to be some swear words which are unrepeatable, but she seemed to see the funny side of things. I was, however, extremely embarrassed.

I became the babysitter to the children of the other families at the picnics as well as looking after Martin all the time. I didn't mind it too much as Martin had someone to play with, but I have to say I did get a bit weary of coping as it seemed it was expected of me. My contribution to the picnics and barbeques used to be a strawberry sponge cake which went down well. Later, when we went to spend time during the holidays or family days at one of the many lakes around Toronto, there would be a large gathering of Cypriots enjoying their lively chatter and making barbeques in their new country. Although I enjoyed being in their company and observing their enjoyment, I found it difficult to converse with or confide in anyone.

At least at the lakes I was able to go for a swim and started getting Martin used to the water. I also helped with the fishing by getting over any squeamishness of fixing the worm bait onto a fishhook for Martin. I don't remember if we ever caught anything.

Occasionally it was decided that we should entertain a couple of families in our apartment, but I never liked it when the women took over my kitchen to make their Greek dishes. I wasn't able to object. They were kind and friendly and meant well so I just had to accept that that was how things were done. Piero invited some young men into our apartment once who dropped their cigarette ash and stubbed the butts out on the Parkay floor which made me angry and upset. They had recently arrived and perhaps didn't know the value of the flooring. This was another reason for an argument which I guess I lost. I spent ages trying to rub the stains out. We were not able to afford a carpet which would probably have prevented the stains and they may not have been so careless. Cigarette ash and butts were always a problem for me as I didn't smoke but Piero could get through about forty a day. Alcohol was never a problem though as neither of us drank, except for the occasional glass of wine when we were with company. It was also an expense we could not afford.

I was never able to have enough money to buy such things as curtains, ironing board, rugs, bedspreads and many other household items. He begrudged me buying any clothing from stockings to material for making clothes. Piero had persuaded me, however, to help buy a little red MGB car by signing an HP agreement. I had objected to the purchase of the car in the first place as I could use public transport to my work and Piero had a company vehicle. It was not really suitable for Toronto weather either. We also definitely did not have enough money, but he was adamant that we should buy it. However, it did mean that I could use it to get to the office and it was quite fun to drive in the summer when the weather was good, and we could have the top down.

When we first got the car, we went for a short holiday to Ottawa but hadn't gone far before we had a minor accident and I experienced Piero having road-rage, so the trip was abandoned. Later we went on a trip to Atlantic City, New Jersey on the fast and dangerous freeway into the United States, little Martin perched in the back behind us. We did have seatbelts and there was a rollbar for safety. It was a lucky thing that we didn't have another, more serious accident. This long trip was taken in order that Piero could go to the Casinos which left me and Martin spending the days walking up and down the boardwalk trying not to spend too much money in cafes. It was a break to stay in a hotel, however, but it wasn't a particularly memorable holiday for me. I hated the way I always felt cheated when I went to buy food at the self-service counters. I would just get through with my tray, pay for the food and go to take my tray to a table, when the tray was whipped out of my hands by a big burly man. It wasn't out of kindness for a mother struggling with a small child and a tray. It was so I would give him the expected tip for taking it to my table.

I found the experience of getting to Atlantic City rather scary as well as we drove through Harlem and there were gangs of men hanging about street corners which made me feel vulnerable in our small car. I think Piero may have felt that way too, so we never stopped. The only part of New York I saw on that trip was the back of the Statue of Liberty.

I eventually gave my notice in to J. H Lock. & Sons. I joined a temping agency and started work in the IT department for The Borden Milk Company at their Home Office in February 1970. They offered me a permanent position after a month. I was to become departmental secretary and personal assistant to the manager of information systems, Doug Smith. One of my jobs was to check and type flow charts for the coders, so I became familiar with computers and computing from the early days. It's a pity I didn't learn coding myself. I was also secretary to the manager of cost analysis and special projects, Tony Gleeson. He would often dictate a letter for me to type right at the end of the day. This could be annoying as I was always anxious not to be late collecting Martin and getting home, but I was earning well, loved my job and the people I worked with. The days were long when I had to leave Martin with a childminder before going to work and then rush home to collect him. I never really got the chance to do the potty training which has always bothered me as a mother. If I was late home, Piero would not be happy.

One good thing about my jobs so far was the amount of experience I was getting and, not having been qualified in accountancy or IT, I was learning on the job. The company, being the home office, also meant that we would make conference calls to the other provinces in Canada, a function at the forefront of technology in 1970. I even learned to spot errors the coders made on their flow-charts so they could be corrected, and I helped create a new filing system for the company. In any case, I was happy with my employment, the salary I was receiving and the prospects of advancement I had there.

Toronto was a fast city. I had very wide roads and a highway called the McDonald Cartier Freeway which was always full of fast-moving traffic. The cold winters brought heavy snow which soon turned black as it was piled up beside the sides of the streets and the hot summers could be unbearable in the city. The surrounding lakes and forests provided a welcome relief in the summer, and everyone went outside to picnic and barbeque. All the parks had excellent facilities for recreation and there was even a zoo. In the winter there were nearby ski slopes and not far from our apartment block there was a skating rink where I would take Martin sometimes. It may have been a busy place, but it was also a lovely city in my view and I particularly liked the light which gave the place a special feel. I think the light was popular with artists. Christmas with all the lights gave it a lovely atmosphere and the malls which were mostly underground were always very handy, particularly the store that sold doughnuts. It was a treat to take Martin to the malls to shop. We were living in a big city and having the big city experience but one which was quite different to London.

We discovered one day that Piero had developed diabetes. Although he was very slim there were signs, we weren't aware of. He needed to have a health check for insurance purposes so went to see a doctor and got the diagnosis. In hindsight, we probably didn't recognize the signs and perhaps because of his Mediterranean diet as a youth, it was kept at bay and wasn't noticed earlier. He quite naturally was terribly upset about this and I felt sorry for him. I tried to help him with his diet by adapting recipes. We tried to go back to that good childhood diet with plenty of fresh vegetables, olives, olive oil but little in the way of sugary things. He was now in his early thirties being eight years older than me. His frustration was obvious, and I trained myself to give him his injections, hoping that would also help with our relationship. However, he continued to ignore the doctor's advice and drank a lot of sugary drinks with several spoons of sugar in his Turkish coffee. I usually made the coffee for him in the traditional manner with a tiny saucepan and I tried reducing the amount of sugar I put in, but it didn't help. He also continued to smoke heavily.

I continued to have fears. Now that I was back in Canada, would my father get wind of where I was living and turn up unannounced? I would always be anxious that he would appear out of a crowd when I was walking in the city. I had heard that he walked across Canada with a dog which didn't help reduce my fears. I also found it a bit difficult to deal with Martin as I had heard that if you are abused, you become an abuser too. It worried me when I was changing his nappy. 'Would I have feelings towards him that weren't proper?' It never happened, of course, but it certainly did play with my mind.

22 - ESCAPE

Our personal life continued to deteriorate. Piero kept on gambling even to the point of coming home in the middle of the night to take money from my purse and return to the card game. After one particular session of playing cards, he lost another 500 dollars or more. Considering that both our weekly wages were less than 100 dollars a week each, I objected, of course, but he got even angrier with me for doing so. He would win and besides, I could earn more. There was no way I could contact my family in England, and I became scared of every move I made in case it upset him. He always discouraged any friends I had. He telephoned one particular girlfriend of mine and called her a whore and one or two other expletives saying she was influencing me. I had to sit quietly in the company of his Cypriot friends and when I began to get bored and tired, he would say I was showing contempt, which wasn't true at all. I was bored and extremely exhausted. I guess I was to be seen and not heard.

I arrived at work some days with bruises which I hoped were well covered with makeup. My brother came to visit briefly in March. During that time Piero put on his charm, he even let me go with my brother to a pop concert on Centre Island. Unfortunately, when we got back Piero had put a large bath towel on Martin instead of one of the diapers, I had left out for him. He made it known that he wasn't happy that I had gone, even with my own brother, even though he had said he didn't object. I think my brother realized something was wrong, though, because he took a photograph of me but there was nothing that he could do about it. As it happened, the photo, being black and white didn't show the bruises, but I do look very gaunt in it.

There was a moment in the depth of winter when I felt I could take no more. I walked out into the snow and just kept going. I couldn't see how I could get out of the situation. I had had the humiliation of being turned down by the landlord of the flat, for an extension to pay the rent as we were in arrears. I found myself begging the woman in charge of collecting the rent and she, understandably, gave me no sympathy. Somehow, I managed to scrape enough together to avoid eviction, but I was exhausted, lacked sleep and had had enough. I just wanted to curl up and die.

Piero followed me to where I had lain down in the snowbank and pulled me back to the flat with his usual promises that things would get better. However, they didn't, and things came to a head in January 1971 when he became extremely violent. He started accusing me of having an affair which I denied. I had been suggesting we might have a separation or seek advice from a marriage guidance counsellor. I ended up being beaten and had a nosebleed in front of Martin. I tried to stem the blood with my dressing gown. He then pulled me by the hair into Martin's bedroom and made Martin sit up while he proceeded to cut my night dress up with scissors saying 'Look at your mummy, she is an f……c… She wants another daddy for you.' 'Look what she's made me do.' I wanted to call an ambulance as I couldn't stop the bleeding. Piero refused to call them, so I had to do it myself. The bleeding stopped shortly after the call, so I had to contact them again to cancel it. My screams and his loud shouting brought neighbours to bang on the door. I escaped into the hallway of the apartment block and refused to go back in fear that he would kill me. He then got Martin out of bed and told him to tell me to come inside. He then came after me into the hall and dragged me by the hair back to our apartment in front of witnesses.

The police came. I escaped into the hallway again and sheltered in a neighbour's flat but went back again when Piero promised the police he would stop. They gave him the address of a marriage guidance counsellor. I didn't press charges. I didn't want to lose my son as Piero had threatened I would, and the police didn't press charges themselves. My neck was hurting badly so the Police offered to take me to the hospital, but Piero promised he would order a taxi and as he had calmed down by then. The policemen left. However, once they were gone, Piero said I could get a taxi if I slept with someone to earn the money to pay for it like a prostitute.

In the months before this, I would often put Martin to bed, read him a story and settle him for the night only for Piero to interrupt and take Martin to watch TV with him. When Martin began to fuss and fret from being over-tired, he would shout at him to be quiet, sit still and call me to put him to bed. Any attempt I made regarding discipline was always contradicted so poor Martin could never tell right from wrong.

One time, while Martin was watching, Piero, in a fit, emptied all the kitchen cupboards and smashed every single breakable thing. He pulled all my clothes out of the cupboards and put them in heap on the floor and proceeded to burn holes in them with his cigarette. He put the TV on full volume and turned all the lights on. When I put Martin back to bed and closed the door, he opened the door again. This was all because of a complaint I probably made about his gambling when he had once again spent his pay packet and I had made a further attempt to suggest we separated.

A day or two after, I received more punches and kicks. I was once again dragged in front of Martin and because I had said that our marriage was definitely at an end, he said that I must have been having an affair. He pulled my wedding ring off and bent my thumb back to breaking point saying that he was going to kill me. He asked me to come and look at the accounts, which I did. He seemed to calm down, so I went and took a shower. When I came out, he was steaming and what happened next was almost indescribable. He had hold of my hair and started shaking me about. He punched me and squeezed my neck. Said he would kill me before the night was out. He took his belt off and started striking me with it. He pinned me down on the sofa and continued punching me. I don't know how I extricated myself and calmed him down. I think he left the flat.

Somehow, I managed to persuade him that I would go back to England to try to get some money from my grandfather. How I managed I don't know but he let me go with Martin. It was the 8th of February 1971. Things had to happen fast. I couldn't give proper notice for my job so left on the 9th of February. However, my boss and colleagues were incredibly supportive, giving me a particularly good reference, a card wishing me luck and an offer of a job again if I ever came back. Some of the staff had witnessed Piero coming to stand outside the office building and abuse me both verbally and physically.

I did receive comforting letter a year later from one of my bosses asking how I was and hoping things were better for me now. It was most kind of him. I may have been sad to leave my friends from High School, but I was also sad to leave my work colleagues in Toronto. They were all such friendly interesting people and I felt at home back in Canada with Canadians.

I had managed to scrape a fare together and I seem to remember my mother had sent me some money. I booked a flight on Air Canada, packed an overnight bag and dressed Martin, who was still only three, in his pyjamas and dressing gown letting him clutch his teddy-bear. Piero drove us to the airport. It was snowing and the roads were covered in ice. He stopped several times, turned back once but changed his mind and carried on to the terminal. All the while he was dragging continuously on a cigarette. It was the longest car journey I had ever taken. I really did not think we would get to the airport. Piero dropped us at the airport, parked the car and joined us to the check-in but he didn't stop us. Martin and I had to move quickly as we were running late but to my great relief we reached and passed through the gate. I still didn't feel completely safe but knew I couldn't be followed. The plane was then delayed for what seemed an eternity, due to ice on the runway. Eventually the plane took off and Martin and I were on our way to start another chapter.

23- I'M PUT TO BED

I remember little about the flight from Toronto except that we had middle seats which meant Martin could sleep comfortably cuddling his teddy bear. When we arrived at Heathrow, we were met by my mother who must have been very worried. It was the 10th of February 1971. I was in such a state that I didn't know what to do, whether I had done the right thing, I just knew I had had to get away. We arrived at Kitchen Hall and my mother put me to bed and dealt with Martin. I guess I must have been having to deal with jetlag as well. However, the next morning my mother took me to the doctor who examined me noting the bruises on my back, thighs and ankle as well as my painful thumb and ring finger. For my mental state he prescribed tranquilizers and I was told to rest. In his statement on my application charging Piero with Persistent Cruelty, Dr. McDonald said I 'was in a very depressed state. Multiple injuries, bruising back head and next extending to base of neck. Cut and bruised lower lip. Bruising inner left wrist and small joints of fingers of right hand and thumb of left hand. Bruise left knee to calf. Compatible with violent physical assault, I think by hand.'

I wrote a letter to Piero explaining that there was no way I was returning to him and the marriage was well and truly over. The letter probably didn't reach him before he had followed me back in England and went to stay with his uncle. I don't remember agreeing to meet him but I may have done so with a member of my family, where he suggested my mother was trying to influence me into not returning to him. I let him know my mind was made up and, on the 17th of February, wrote another letter to him saying that I was going away for a few days and he should only communicate with me through my lawyers, Stanley Tee & Co. I gave him their telephone number.

I went into hiding with Martin. My mother's cousin and

godmother Geraldine and her husband, who lived near Windsor, kindly offered to put us up. Being there I felt safe knowing the address would not be revealed to Piero. I have always been grateful for their help. We had a nice break staying with them and we even went to see the Queen and the Duke of Edinburgh when they attended the Easter church service at Windsor.

I immediately applied to the Harlow Justices Court for a separation order and was awarded custody of Martin on the grounds of Piero's persistent cruelty. My doctor gave evidence of the bruising and swelling on my fingers and my mother made a statement about my distressed condition on returning to England. It would mean that Piero would not be permitted to live with me or pester me in any way. If he did, I could go straight back to court. I was to be paid £1 per year in respect of maintenance for myself and £1 for the maintenance of Martin. This was never, ever received. Piero had pleaded destitution. I couldn't start divorce proceedings, however, as I had not been resident back in England long enough.

While I waited for the court order to come through, it was agreed that Piero could see Martin for a few hours once a week. I allowed him to take Martin as per the agreement and my mother handed Martin over so there would be no confrontation for me. Martin was brought back again. It seemed to be working.

On the 6th of March, my mother was going to London on business so agreed to take Martin to meet Piero at Hangar Lane in order for them to visit London Zoo. She was to collect him from Waterloo Station at 6 o'clock in the evening. However, he didn't appear, and my mother had to come home without Martin.

I was totally devastated, and I became desperate. My poor mother was terribly distressed too, having to bring me such news. However, my mother was a practical person and calmed me down. We had to consider what action we needed to take. I thought maybe Martin had been taken to stay with one of Piero's uncles in London, but we heard nothing.

It's difficult to describe how distraught I was, yet worse was to come. On the 14th of March, I received a telegram from Nicosia in Cyprus: "*MARTIN VERY ILL, PLEASE COME. STOP. TICKET AT BEA W. LONDON TERMINAL. Signed Piero.*"

Figure 28: The Telegram

Well, you can imagine what that did to me. I had to believe Martin was ill. I couldn't contain myself or think straight and was once again prescribed tranquilizers by my doctor. I must have been a bit irrational because I was worried that I would become addicted to the drugs. I asked my doctor about it and he told me that as soon as I had my son with me again, I would forget about any tablets.

My mother and I tried and managed to telephone the hospital in Nicosia, but they didn't have any knowledge of any child being admitted by the name we gave. However, a few hours later, Piero's brother, Andros telephoned me and said that Martin was not ill, but would I come to Cyprus to be reconciled with Piero. This I could not do. I just could not think straight. I eventually calmed down with the thought that Piero's mother Elektra, a woman I respected, would probably look after Martin well while I decided how to proceed. The tranquilizers may also have been working. I realized that nothing could happen fast, so I joined an agency and found another temping job to keep sane and also to prove I could look after Martin on my own.

I wrote to the Chief Welfare Officer in Nicosia, explaining the problem and how concerned I was for the welfare of Martin and that I had asked for Martin to be returned because I was afraid of Piero and couldn't come to Cyprus for that reason. The Harlow Magistrate's court order was made on the 18th of March and I had the separation order and custody of Martin. Harlow Magistrates Court also sent copies of the order to the Registrar in the District Court of Nicosia. I received a letter back from them to say they would look into the matter and contact me 'in due course' and had referred it to the Cyprus High Commission in London. It happened that Piero's uncle worked for the High Commission. Martin was only on my passport, so I guess this relationship may have helped Piero to have Martin added to his passport.

On the 27th of March I received a letter from Piero in Cyprus in which he said that he wanted a reconciliation and that if I didn't come to Cyprus to try living with him again, with promises that I wouldn't have to work and he would put money in an account for me, he was going to take Martin away with him to an undisclosed place and I wouldn't see him again. He also promised that he would take good care of Martin if that happened. If, however I came, tried living with him again and then decided to leave, he would accept that. He had been to see a lawyer and had been advised.

Martin's birthday was on the 21st of March, so I missed his 4th birthday which was extra hard for me.

24 - I GO TO CYPRUS

After I had received the separation order and custody of Martin, I started to find out about going to Cyprus to go through the court there and get Martin back into my custody. With the help of my mother and grandfather, who provided me with some funding as well as support, we found a friend of the family who had a house in the northern part of Cyprus. The Guy-Wrights of Hallingbury, offered to let me and my brother Jon stay there while details were sorted out. My grandparents also came out to have a holiday and stayed in a hotel in Kyrenia, Northern Cyprus. We found a lawyer in Nicosia who agreed to take the case. His name was Christos Christophides who was in fact engaged to an English girl.

On the 1st of April 1971 we flew to Nicosia. My brother was taking time off from his university degree course so couldn't stay with me for long. We did look into ways of escape that I might take if the court case went against me - that was by taking a sailing boat with someone we befriended who had his boat in the harbour. It was an alternative escape route but thank goodness we never had to take up that option. Many people whom I met in Cyprus at the time heard about the 'tug of love' case. Most of them were very friendly and helpful. I guess it might have found its way into the newspapers but being in Greek, I couldn't read them.

My lawyer informed me that the first thing I had to do in order to have Martin stay with me while everything was going through court, was to have him made the equivalent of a 'chattel,' and I would also have to have a place of my own where he could stay with me. Arrangements for Piero to have access would also have to be established and Martin would have to attend the local kindergarten. I found a suitably comfortable apartment in Eleftherias Street, Kyrenia, with Julia Macrides, a very friendly and helpful landlady. I would not be able to take job as I couldn't obtain a visa. Luckily, I was able to receive a weekly sum from my grandfather from the trust. I am forever grateful for having had such support from my family. Piero had a lot of support from his family. Once I agreed to meet up with his mother, Elektra, outside the courthouse in Nicosia, but she only wished to try and get us to have reconciliation. She couldn't understand why I wouldn't try. I told her it was not possible. It seems that he had made sure his family believed that that was all he wanted.

So, the process began. The Court in Nicosia was right next to the famous Ledra Palace Hotel which was located in the 'Green Zone,' between the Greek Cypriot and Turkish Cypriot part of Nicosia, now located in what was to become a 'buffer zone' between the Turkish North and the Greek Cypriot south. Before the Turkish invasion in 1974 it was already a 'no go' zone for Greek Cypriots.

The quickest way to get from Kyrenia to Nicosia at that time was by joining a United Nations convoy through Turkish held territory. This route was mostly open for foreigners to take. We had to be ready to join the convoy at 8 am and return by 6 pm. If we missed it, we had to take the long way, like the Greek Cypriots, which followed a difficult route along the coast. My brother and I hired a car and joined the convoy. It was a very dusty drive and extremely hot, particularly in the car without air conditioning. We tried to stop so I could use a toilet, which was not approved of as we needed to keep in the convoy, but we did try for a quick break. I stayed in the car while my brother checked the café out, but he came running back to the car to say that we must go quickly as the Turkish proprietor had offered to buy me. I did have long blonde hair at the time, but it certainly scared us. I didn't wish to be kidnapped to add to the difficulties. I wondered just what sort of country I had come to. It was a scary time for us as we were not used to military presence with guards and rifles at the ready. We were told there were snipers about in the hills. However, over time I grew to really like Cyprus and the people there. They were not all like my husband and I would tell them so. I really did like Piero's family, particularly Elektra who held down two jobs while living in England having brought up five children. The family came to England in about 1960 as migrants from Cyprus and lived in the Camden area of London before moving to Harlow. Elektra worked in the clothing industry while Piero and Lakis attended colleges. Most of the family moved back to Cyprus before the Turkish invasion in 1974. They lived in Othonos Street, right in the middle of Nicosia.

I had to attend the court several times over the next three months. I would sit in the courtyard and crochet and knit continuously as a way to keep my patience. I could never understand what was being said. I couldn't grasp even the basic words in Greek, which was spoken with speed, helped along with a lot of gesticulating. It was necessary for me to rely on a translation from my lawyer. It continued to be a traumatic time for me, and my brother had to return to university, so I made the trip from Kyrenia to Nicosia with my lawyer over the long route several times as he lived in Kyrenia too. He asked me if I had any advice about mixed marriages as he and his fiancé were planning to marry, and he wished me to meet her. I assured them that my problem was with Piero and that not everyone was like him. They invited me to their wedding which was in a lovely little white church up in the hills and I helped my landlady, who was their friend, put together the decorations such as the little bags of almonds and sachets of lavender, a couple of which I still have today. It was a lovely experience which helped to temper the trauma.

Piero tried to go for reconciliation. I adamantly refused as my whole purpose of being in Cyprus was to get Martin back, particularly as I was convinced that I was the most capable to give him better life back in England. Piero used everything he could to prove that I was an unfit mother. He even used his knowledge of my previous problem with my father as a way of proving that I was unfit. I was quite sickened by this and really worried that the Court would listen to him. I had no idea how the Court would react. Would they blame me for what had happened in my childhood? What had he told them? I found this was particularly cruel. I had obtained character references from my headmistress, Joyce Bowis in Peterborough as well as Doctor Booth, my grandparents' and my mothers' doctor, who attended my birth. He vouched for the character of my family. I also produced copies of my references from my former employers in Canada. My grandfather offered me a position in the farm office which meant that I could tell the court that I had a permanent and secure job to return to in England. It was a great opportunity for me so I sent a letter to my employers in Harlow to thank them for holding my job open but that I would not be returning. They were very understanding too, but I hadn't really worked for them for more than a few months.

When I first saw Martin after I was given access, I was totally shocked. He had a lovely head of curls which I would trim but now all his hair had been shaved off and he looked a couple of years older than he was. He also looked very pale and appeared quiet and confused. It was more than heart-breaking for me.

I took Martin to the little school in Kyrenia each day and on weekends he was picked up by relatives of Piero so he could be

 with his father at weekends. Each time he came back to me was difficult as he couldn't understand why I wouldn't go back to his father who made so many promises.

He continued to press for reconciliation.

Figure 29: Martin with me in Kyrenia

25- LIVING IN CYPRUS

Kyrenia was a beautiful town with a harbour and a mountainous backdrop. I spent a lot of time on the beach with Marin enjoying the wonderful sunshine, sea and sand. While my grandparents were staying, we went on trips to the hills and mountains and had picnics with delicious Cyprus potatoes and slices of ham. It was a colourful place too. The smell of lemons pervaded in villages such as Lapethos and we visited various ruins such as the monastery at Bellapais. There was a unit of United Nations soldiers there with their pale blue berets playing contemporary music particularly 'In the summertime' by Mungo Jerry, and there was always a donkey living on the roof of the ruined castle. There were outside cafes where men would sit drinking Turkish coffee and playing a version of backgammon. The women would perch themselves in the squares sewing and nattering. They always sought to make a fuss of Martin. I also enjoyed the Greek food and would often buy a lamb kebab in a flat bread wrap, *souvlaki*, to share with Martin along with a fresh salad and olives.

We were lucky enough to be invited to the harbour carnival as guests of the harbour master which I was grateful for, and I felt honoured. I had heard some of the competitors practice their singing from their flats in our street getting ready for their competition. I made a couple of ex-pat friends with children the same age as Martin. Everyone was kind and always had a special word for Martin. They appeared to love children. Once, when I was in a shop, the owner introduced me to a well-known politician in Cyprus who was in there at the same time. He wished me good luck. I was even offered a job to be a companion to the wife of an English couple who were returning to Dubai. They suggested I could be a part-time nanny and help home-school their children and I would be safe from Piero there. I didn't fancy living in such a closed community, unable to drive outside the 'compound' even though they offered me good accommodation and good pay. Besides, I had already accepted a job in the office of my grandfather's business. I have to say, I always have mixed emotions about Cyprus, which I suppose is hardly surprising.

There was an hilarious incident which occurred one day when Martin and I were in the flat which had a balcony over the street. I was in the kitchen and Martin was playing in the living room, or so I thought. I suddenly heard a lot of laughing in the street. I ran out on to the balcony to see what was happening and there was my little son doing a wee over the edge. I reprimanded him of course and was embarrassed, to say the least, but the humour of the situation was evident in the street below. It gave the locals something to laugh about – that 'English girl with her little boy.' I am sure that Martin will not mind that I mention this incident. It was one of the lighter moments in our lives.

I penned a short story many years later, recalling my time waiting for a verdict from the Cypriot court and have decided to place it here to give an insight into how I felt during that time.

######### A Short Story............

My Wait

I stepped out of the taxi at ten minutes to ten, on time as usual and only because I had ordered my transport a good hour before I needed to leave. Local time, as I had learned and had now become accustomed to, meant being consistently late and late I did not intend to be.

The sun was already extremely hot on the gravel courtyard as I walked purposefully towards the entrance. It was the end of May and during the three months I had been living in the Island, each clear day had become progressively warmer. As I neared the well-worn stone steps, I wondered how long I would have to wait today.

"Patience" I muttered under my breath. "Patience. This will have to end soon. This waiting."

A smart secretary, dressed in a simple royal blue suit, sun-bleached white blouse, and black shoes with just a hint of height, tripped quickly across the courtyard. Her long dark hair was tied back in a neat chignon and her arms were full of documents. She gave me a pleasant but knowing smile as she passed.

"Kali mera," she said.

"Good ... kali mera," I answered.

Once through the huge arched doorway of the building, I again found herself in the vast room with stone columns. My shoes made a loud clunking noise as I walked across the highly polished marble floor towards the old wooden bench. Here I would sit, alone as usual. Occasionally someone would walk through from the courtyard where everyone else did their waiting. I, being an outsider, could never feel comfortable there. Sometimes another woman, a mother or grandmother, clothed in the traditional long black dress with black headscarf, would stand by my bench to wait for an errant son or husband. They had usually come to pay bail or to wail about an unfair verdict.

Today the room felt cold compared to the heat outside and I knew I would be glad of the coolness by the end of the day if I she had to wait that long.

Settling myself on the hard seat I reached into my shopping basket that contained a lunch box, unfinished sewing, reading material and legal documents. I pulled out some wool and a crochet hook. Since all this court business had started, I had found that the best way to keep sane and calm was to spend my hours crocheting and so, suitably equipped, I resigned myself to the waiting game.

Voices could be heard coming from behind the huge thick courtroom doors. To me they sounded like arguments and I visualized the gestures, the waving of arms and the nodding of heads, that were all part of the diction of the language I had never been able to master. I felt very isolated in that large spacious room – that hollow echoing place. I had become a lost soul, conspicuous in my summer dress and my fair hair combed up into a ponytail. When anyone walked by, I had the feeling they wanted to avoid me at all costs, and any smile they displayed was only a token smile. A civil smile. I imagined everyone knew my reason for being here. They had already made their judgment. After all, the case had reached the local gossip columns.

I waited; I crocheted; I read passages from books. Any time now my advocate, Mr. Christophides, or a clerk of the court would emerge from one of the courtrooms to tell me it was all over. A verdict would have been reached. It would be in my favour and I could go home.

The voices gabbled on. A typist tapped away on an old manual typewriter in one of the side offices and, now and then, a chair scraped. The huge clock, tacked precariously on to one of the columns, ticked on, and my waiting space seemed to expand. I began to experience the familiar sensation of becoming small and insignificant. A shrivelling plum. A tiny waif in a vast arena. I felt as though all the walls were lined with eyes that were watching me, waiting for me to crumble. I had cried enough. I had to be tough. I had to be patient.

At twelve o'clock things began to stir. Smartly dressed men in shirts and ties, all carrying briefcases, made their way through the waiting room and out into the courtyard for the lunch break. Their siesta. Maybe they would come back again at half past three for a couple of hours, maybe not. It seemed I just had to wait a bit longer. The dapper Mr. Christophides came out from behind one of the many doors and walked over to me. He was a handsome, tall man with a pleasant voice. He smiled kindly as he told me that there was going to be a bit of delay but that he was sure things would be sorted out in the afternoon session. I would have to come back after lunch.

Not surprised by this announcement, I got up to stretch her legs then went outside for a walk around the yard, feeling dreadfully self-conscious. I walked a little way up a nearby street where, it being mid-day, I found all the doors and windows shuttered. Every now and then I could hear people talking and clinking cutlery. Someone laughed. A dog barked. A child cried. I saw no-one. After a while I strolled back to the courthouse to get out of the heat and to use the facilities.

It was while washing my face in the huge courthouse basin that I had a sudden flash of memory. Perhaps it was the coldness of the water or the whiteness of the washroom tiles, but I found myself in another place, another life, another world. Perhaps it was in another universe, but it was all very vivid.

I was in a land of snow and ice. Children were tumbling out of a school dressed in thick parkas with gloves and rubber boots. They were lining up to walk two abreast in the snow. It was Christmas and the whole school was on its way to sing carols at the small wooden church in town. It was a western Canadian frontier town where most of the children had been bussed into school from outlying farms and rural pick-up points. Many would have walked several miles and now they were off down the hill, full of excitement about the seasonal celebrations.

I allowed myself to indulge in the vision, the feel of the cold and the fun of the snow. I could see the classes, six in all, slipping and sliding down the slope into town. One class was led by Miss Marsh. Prim, strict, middle-aged, unmarried Miss Marsh. Then it happened. Miss Marsh slipped. She fell headfirst into the snowbank; her legs flailed the air and her heavy woollen skirt lifted to reveal the biggest pair of pantaloons I had ever seen. I remembered Miss Marsh's brilliant red face as she regained her footing to the taunts of the sniggering boys. I remembered telling the tale to my mother that evening and my mother's reply: - "That must have been a sight for sore eyes!"

The sound of church bells brought me back from my daydreaming. I dried my hands and face, put a little make-up on, then went back to the bench to carry on with the waiting.

Gradually the building began to buzz with life as the afternoon sessions got underway and Mr. Christophides breezed through with a smile and a nod. He looked noticeably confident and I felt reasonably reassured.

'Maybe this **will** be my last day here' I thought, 'and one day I'll write all this down!'

And now, at last, I am writing it all down.

……… **End of Story**…………

Finally, the day came on the 4th of June 1971 when the Cypriot court in Nicosia gave me custody of Martin and he was to reside with me in England. *'If Pieris continued to live in Cyprus, Martin was to go there to spend no more than 2 months during the summer, timed to coincide with school holidays so as not to interfere with his schooling and the fare to be paid for by Pieris. If Pieris moved to England he was to have access every weekend, Saturday overnight to Sunday. Martin was to be brought up in the Greek Orthodox religion and Pieris was to decide his education so long as he paid the cost, otherwise Martin should go to the local school by agreement with his mother. The agreement was to*

come into effect on 18th June to give time for the arrangements
to be communicated to the Cyprus High Commission in London.'

I was so relieved. I had almost resigned myself to the decision that if the case went against me, I would not try to get Martin back anymore. I wanted him to have a settled life and maybe it would have been okay to be with his Cypriot family after all the trauma, even though I was convinced he would be better off with me.

Martin and I returned to England after nearly three months.

Tug of Love

She knitted once.
Her needles beat a retreat
from the real world,
gave her hope to face the un-faceable.

She knitted once.
Knitting tempered the pain,
gave her strength to cope
with custody hearings in a foreign court.

She knitted once
in the heat of a Cyprus spring
knitted up her patience
waiting for her child's return.

(Spring 1971 - Cyprus) 11.09.98

26- BACK TO ENGLAND

At last Martin and I returned to England. It was wonderful to be back home with my family even though it was going to have to be temporary. We moved into that lovely house called Kitchen Hall Farm to be with my mother and younger brother and sisters. Almost straight away I went to work in the New Hall Farm office to take up the job my grandfather had offered me. It was summertime now, so Martin stayed at Kitchen Hall and my mother or younger brother helped to look after him. My mother also worked part time with my grandfather and did the wages.

Kitchen Hall Farm was bought by my grandfather to add to his acreage at New Hall Farm which was next door. The elderly couple who lived in it before us had reduced themselves to using just one room and kitchen so it had to have some work done on it before my mother could move in from the house at Hastingwood. It was purported to have been a kitchen to a monastery because of its name and after several layers of different fireplaces were removed, at the coaxing of my Aunt Molly and Uncle Austen, a lovely inglenook fireplace appeared. It was a Grade II listed building because of its age and position with a pond and willow trees in the garden. Kitchen Hall house, which may once have been moated, retains the central range and service cross wing of an early 17th-century building but there are some 19th-century additions. It became a perfect family home where in later years all my brothers and sisters, their children and even grandchildren were able to visit and covet. We also discovered that the house, part of the original Manor of Kitchen Hall was listed in the Domesday Book.

There was a farm track over the fields between the two farms passing a wood called Barnsley's, a distance of about a mile and a half. In the summer it was a lovely walk to take and I have so many fond memories of the place.

I was enthusiastic about my new job, particularly as it was for my own family and now, I wanted to give something back to my grandfather for all the help he had given me over the years. I started with answering the phone and soon learned everything about the market garden business, the rose growing business and the arable business. There were actually two if not three businesses involved. One was for the growing of the crops such as potatoes, cabbage, lettuce, rhubarb, sprouts and other similar seasonal vegetables, as well as the arable crops of wheat, barley, tic beans and, eventually, oilseed rape. One was the wholesale fruit and vegetable outlet where we sent farm-grown produce on a fleet of lorries to the London markets of Borough, Covent Garden and Spitalfields and returned with items for the local greengrocers and merchants. The third was the growing in rotation with the other crops, of over a quarter of a million bare root roses, floribundas, hybrid teas and standard bushes for the wholesale market. For me, the job got busier and busier.

I got to know my grandfather better too. To me he was special and someone whom I could trust though no word was ever spoken about my history. He gave me every opportunity at work, and I like to think I gave much back. Every couple of weeks he would go to Chelmsford Assises as he was a JP (Justice of the Peace) and I was proud of the fact that he was considered and had been invited to be one. At that time, a JP was usually someone of standing in the community who was offered the post.

My 'grandpa' seemed to be popular with the workers on the farm and I think he was very generous yet firm and not at all judgmental. I remember one incident which I think amused him. He was driving me somewhere in his fairly new car and we ran out of fuel. He had a can in the boot but when we got it out, we discovered there was no funnel with it. He started suggesting that one of us would have to walk to a garage to see if we could get hold of a funnel, but I said that I had an idea. On the back seat was a magazine, most likely *The Farmers' Weekly*. I took the magazine, folded it into a makeshift funnel and we were able to pour the fuel through it. Maybe the fact I had been brought up on a farm where everything was makeshift, had given me the idea but it was good to find my 'grandpa' saying he was proud of me.

27- I BECOME ESTABLISHED

Meanwhile I applied to rent a council house in Harlow, and I moved with Martin to 13 The Fortunes near Bush Fair. I hoped the number thirteen was a good omen and it turned out that it was. The house was in a row of terraces situated near to the shops with footpaths to the Town Centre and handy to the bus route. There were also schools nearby as well as a pub called the Poplar Kitten. One of the many pubs in Harlow New Town named after a butterfly. It was ideal for me and Martin as it had two bedrooms and a decent sized garden so we could eventually have a kitten for him. We also made room for a budgie which he loved, and it was such a pleasure for me to have somewhere for us to settle in properly.

Not long after I moved there, I joined the Eighteen Plus group so that I could meet other singles like myself. I enrolled Martin in the school and found a childminder. Because I was working for family, it was a bit easier for me to get time off if I needed as I could make my hours up later. I could even take work home if necessary. I was able to use one of the farm cars, which was extremely helpful, so I didn't need to use public transport. Although there were buses in the town, they were a bit limited for getting to the farm.

At the beginning of July, shortly after returning from Cyprus and before I had moved to a new house, I received a phone call from Piero asking me to let him have Martin for two hours on Saturday as he was going away. He had obviously returned to England. I allowed him to have Martin and I think my mother was with me when I handed Martin over. He brought Martin back. It was an uncomfortable time but had to be done. I asked him where he was going to live but he didn't wish to tell me. He then asked if I would send Martin to Canada for two weeks the following summer, but when I said I couldn't give him an answer straight away, he said I would have to send Martin to Cyprus as per the agreement and that he would 'take it from there.' I asked him to send me the fares first. He wrote a letter to my mother apologizing for the trouble he had caused, and to me he said he would send me a weekly sum. He would send me his address and asked for a weekly report on Martin.

Piero was never given my home address and all correspondence with Piero was done through my mother's address. There was no way I wished to have him turn up on my doorstep. Even so, I started to feel anxious as I didn't know where he was or when he would turn up and at the back of my mind I still worried that my father would try to contact me or appear out of nowhere. I had had that fear for the last seven years, even though I knew my father was not allowed to enter the UK.

I had to wait a year before I could start divorce proceedings and I also needed to have an address for Piero. I was advised by my solicitor that I shouldn't allow Martin to go to Canada and it was also doubtful if I needed to send Martin to Cyprus should Piero return there, as he had already left and come to the UK, all in accordance with the court order from Nicosia. In the meantime, I did receive some erratic payments of maintenance for a few months at the end of 1973 and beginning of 1974 from Piero in Canadian dollars so at least that was something.

My life did get a lot better now that I had a place to live and worked for my family as well as having people I could visit with Martin, and he could see his grandmother, step grandfather and great grandparents. He would often come with me to the farm when he was on his holidays from school.

The club I belonged to organized outings and meetings. When I got involved, I found that the club also held coffee mornings so one day I asked my grandmother's good friend, Margaret Milroy, from her university days in Edinburgh, to give us a talk on her travels. She was a remarkably interesting woman and had travelled alone to many different places around the world in her retirement. Places like Tibet and Mongolia I would describe her as an intrepid traveller and her talk and slide shows always went down well. Margaret became a close friend of all the family and was almost like a great aunt to us. It felt good to have been able to contribute to the club.

I made a few friends in the club and did meet one or two men. I started to enjoy having friendships again. There was a neighbour whose daughter came to babysit which was useful. I was back with a life ahead of me. I was also able to start saving. What a joy it was when I had saved enough to buy a lovely new rug for the living room. Prior to that, I had had to make do with second-hand furniture. At last, I was having a normal life.

Next on the list for the club was an organized dance. We hired a hall at North Weald, which just happened to be the same hall where my parents met when my father was billeted at Norway House with other Norwegians during the war. We arranged the music, a bar and food, and took turns behind the bar. While I was on duty, a tall man walked up to order a drink for him and his friends. We chatted and he asked me if I would like a lift home after the dance. I accepted and climbed into his Volkswagen Beetle which had a painting of Donald Duck on it. The man was to be my future husband, John. I had found new love and it was an exciting time. The date will never be forgotten. It was the 21st of September 1971. I was nearly twenty-five years old and Martin was four and a half.

John lived with his parents in Takely and would come to visit me on the weekends. On his first visit, knowing that I was Canadian, he brought me a Leonard Cohen record as well as flowers. I guess I was impressed. We continued to see each other for several months and my life with Martin became regular and routine. I would say that at last I was very content.

At the end of October, I had a request from Piero to see Martin, but I wasn't happy as I had no idea where he was living, and he didn't wish to tell me. I explained that I was going to court to sort out any access and a summons would be served so he could attend the court. The court would decide. Nothing more happened until April 1972, when I started to petition for a divorce. Unfortunately, it had to be held over as Piero had left the address that he had eventually given us and went back to either Canada or Cyprus. I was less anxious even though I didn't know his whereabouts as I knew that he could be arrested if he tried to harass me or turn up unannounced and, besides this, Martin had been made a ward of court and couldn't be taken out of the country again.

I had an ongoing problem with tackling my experiences, though. I always felt that I had managed to forget my history with my father and a lot was put to the back of my mind. I felt that I was getting on with my life and now that I was free from Piero's control as well, reasoned that I could handle it.

Unfortunately, one day I was walking with John by some stalls and tents at an exhibition or an awareness campaign of some sort in Harlow, near the Sports Centre, when I came across particular cause. On the side of the tent was a sign which read 'Survivors.' As I looked at the information board, I gradually began to understand what it was all about. I began to feel clammy. My heart started palpitating. I just had to get away from the tent and leave the area quickly. I don't think I told John what the trouble was, but the issue of child abuse started to appear in all the newspapers. So, where I had thought that what happened to me had been unique, I suddenly discovered that lots of other girls had or were going through the same experience as me. I learned that I was one of them. I learned that I was a survivor. I had never thought of myself as a *survivor*. I had just accepted that I had escaped the abusive relationships and it was all well behind me. Now I had to be reminded over and over as the issues expanded through the newspapers and television programs. I had been a victim of sexual abuse as well as domestic abuse.

I had never heard of such a thing as therapy and thought that I could just plough on leaving my history behind me. I was still determined to handle it myself and never sought to talk to anyone about it. However, as the years went by, I grew ever angrier and sadder that such abuse had happened to me and was being experienced by so many children and women and even men.

When I heard that my father had moved to Norway and had married to a woman younger than my youngest sister, I vowed that if I ever found out that Greta had given birth to a girl, I would write and tell her what had been done to me. As it happened, they had three sons and no daughter. I now had three wonderful Norwegian half-brothers, Ingemar, Johannes and Kristofer who is younger than my youngest daughter by three weeks.

It was to take many years for me to come to terms with both of my experiences at the hands of a controlling man. I'm not sure I have really completely done so. I took to running marathons as my form of therapy and eventually started writing poetry which often sent me into my past. I also found that I had blocked out a lot of what happened to me and it was when I started writing my stories and particularly my poems that memories sprung back for me to tackle.

Perhaps taking up running and writing was the best thing to have done.

28- MARRIAGE AND MOVES

Martin and I got on with our lives. I was keen to get back to some sort of exercise. I tried out with a local basketball team, but found I was too rusty and lacked fitness. John came to stay quite often but it couldn't be permanent as it was a council house and restricted. He remained living with his parents. Communication was difficult too as we didn't have mobile phones then. Once, when I hadn't heard from John for a couple of weeks, I began to wonder if I ever would, so I drove to the address he had given me in Takely, near Great Dunmow. Martin came with me. I didn't want to be left in limbo. When I arrived, it was the first time, I'd met his parents. It turned out that John had a serious case of flu and hadn't been able to get in touch with me. Our relationship continued, I'm glad to say.

As I had been a runner, we decided to jog around the block together. It was a shock to see how unfit I was even for the short distance of about a mile. We decided to continue and one day while visiting and jogging around Hatfield Heath, we came across a strange event. A group of people were running through the woodland with maps and compasses. They were wearing light weight clothing and long socks with shinpads and all seemed to be concentrating extremely hard on routes they were following. They also looked fit, refreshed and were obviously having fun. We approached a couple and sked what it was all about. They invited us to join them in a few weeks' time at an event in Suffolk where they lived. We joined their club called SOS (Suffolk Orienteering Society) and from then on, spent most of our weekends attending events in the forests and parks in Essex and neighbouring counties. We found that the system involved of setting people off at specified times and in different age bands, suited us. It meant that there was always someone able to stay and look after Martin while the other one was taking part. I progressed through the stages and took part in the Open class for people over eighteen until I reached the next age band. I managed to reach a silver standard and finally I actually won a trophy for the Southern Championships where I was given my prize by Chris Brasher. He was the man who started organizing the London Marathon in 1981. So, I started my running career training for not only orienteering events, but also for marathons, half-marathons and 10-kilometre races, all the while mulling over my life. This choice of therapy seemed to be working.

My divorce came through and we were finally able to get married on 28th December 1974 with the wind howling and the rain pelting down. We 'tied the knot' at the Epping Registry Office and had our small and intimate reception at Kitchen Hall Farm. Auntie Marjorie provided me with some lovely flowers, I wore a cream-coloured dress, and my mother produced a meal for all who could attend. John's parents, his brothers Keith with his wife Lynn, Nigel, John's best friend John Sydall with his wife Alison, my mother, stepfather Ray, my brother William and of course Martin were there to witness the occasion. The next day we set off for our honeymoon to Swanage in Dorset. The local newspaper announcement stated that I was a nurse but where they got that idea from, I have yet to find out.

Figure 30: John and My wedding day December 1974

We then started looking into the possibility of buying a house together. This would take time as we needed to save with the building society, not only a decent sum but it was also necessary to prove we had been saving for over a year before they would consider giving us a mortgage. We looked for a place in the surrounding area, not too far from the farm but also near to where John worked as a telephone engineer. We found a detached house in Bishop's Stortford, right in the middle of town but up an extremely steep hill. 69 Newtown Road. It may have been small house, but it suited our needs. We soon made a few alterations, improved the garden, placed a chain fence along the boundary, installed a new post-box, painted it red, and settled in.

John's work headquarters were originally based in Sawbridgeworth when he started but moved to premises next to the train station in Bishop's Stortford. This was ideal for him as he could just walk down the hill to his work each morning. He was also able to go to the local swimming pool in his lunch break or even had time for a run to nearby Hatfield Forest and back.

We enjoyed living in that market town with its quaint shops and Saturday market. I would often meet a friend for a coffee in *Laura Ashley's* in the high street. We had friends, mostly ones that John had acquired before we met, and we would often meet up in one of the local pubs. My favourite drink was a schooner of sherry and also at that time, there was still no drink and drive legislation, so we often went to places like Hatfield Broad Oak for our Sunday lunch. As John's parents lived in nearby Takely, we often went to visit them as well. Sometimes we would go to Kitchen Hall on a Sunday to have lunch with my mother and other members of the family. We always had a great time when there were a lot of us gathered together to celebrate an occasion. However, we never had the opportunity to go for a cross-country ski trip on Christmas morning as we had done in Canada. Instead, it was a cross-country run, usually for John as he would run along the River Stort tow path from our home to Harlow.

When Martin started secondary school, we found him a place at Hadham Hall, not far from Bishop's Stortford, where he played rugby. There was a school bus service which was helpful. After school he would visit with friends or stay with a childminder until we got home. On one occasion he was playing on some equipment in the local park when he fell, and an ambulance had to be called. It was a scary moment for me as I arrived just as he was being carted off and he kept saying 'Don't worry mum. I will be alright.' In the end he was alright but had to have several stitches put into a gash on his forehead.

I continued to commute to the farm at Harlow and on weekends we found ourselves joining the local running club or venturing out to a forest or park to orienteer.

29- MY RUNNING DAYS

Running has always been my 'life-line' and was perhaps the best therapy I could have taken. All the running and athletics I did at school and through high school probably gave me a good grounding in training and fitness. Perhaps I have always felt the need to prove myself in some way and that has been why I have done so much running. I have composed many poems on the theme of running but I have also written about my first London Marathon. I have included my story here. I don't remember writing it but while I was going through a folder which included certificates of various races and fun runs, I found this 'essay' tucked in behind the official photo of me crossing the finishing line with my arms raised showing my relief at reaching the end.

………………A Short Story…………………………

My Enjoyable but Painful Marathon

Written shortly after running my first London Marathon 9th May 1982

I remember reading about the marathon runners when I was about 12 years old and thinking what an amazing accomplishment it must be for any man to be able to run such distances. The idea that a woman could do it never entered my head, the farthest I had ever run was 220 yards and by the time I left high school 440 yards was the maximum for women.

Well, here we are, a dozen or more years later and my teenage dreams have come true. I ran a Marathon, and the sense of achievement was even greater than I had imagined it would be. I was one of the lucky ones as this was a special Marathon for the people, not just the Olympic athletes, and it was a chance for anyone of any ability to try their hand (leg) at an ultra-distance.

Every runner/jogger wanted to enter, and it seemed nearly everyone tried. However, I was entered and my training which had been sporadic until I was notified, began to overtake my evenings.

My programme was basically only plain running ever increasing distances but with the long one each week reserved for Sundays. In February I caught a cold and had to stop training for about two weeks. I got back into full swing a week or so later and finally at four weeks before the big day I ran a comfortable fifteen miles of road and cross country. I followed this the next Sunday with a Half Marathon that went very well so I was getting confident that I would be able to complete the marathon and with the hopeful time of about 4 to 4 1/2 hours. However, my confidence was shattered when a few days later my left knee gave out - too much running on hard surfaces I guess, so I had to stop training and went for one or two gentle jogs during the last week before the 9th of May.

The day drew nearer, and I was very apprehensive about my knee, but in the end, I thought I would run anyway and if it caused too much trouble I would just have to concede to defeat. I was also running in aid of the St. John's Ambulance Cadets and every mile completed would be worth £7.50.

The day arrived and I went with my husband, who had unfortunately not been entered, by taxi to Charring Cross Station. We had stayed the night in London to save a long journey in the morning. We climbed on the train and packed like sardines in a tin, we travelled to Greenwich Station hardly being able to move. I was already experiencing the crowds, and everyone was in high spirits masking the nervousness underneath. The smell of liniment was particularly strong. The weather was fine, perhaps a bit hot, but I didn't mind that, and I intended to drink little and often which in the event I did.

Finally, having put my clothes on the bus, and having queued at the longest loo in the world, I joined the massive start by lining up with the section hoping to run the distance in 4-41/2 hours. I fell in with a Welsh girl who had run a marathon before, and she was to remain my companion for the next 15 miles.

The gun went off and four minutes later we crossed the start line and were on our way. We went carefully at first, warming up and getting into stride which luckily, we found suited both of us and we watched the clock. After about two miles we were running at about 8 ½ minute mile pace which seemed okay, but I found that I was gradually quickening my pace now that I had warmed up, but Linda kept me in check for which I was glad as it was so easy to get carried away.

The spectators were wonderful, and they made us feel as though we were the only individuals in the race that mattered. Even after only two miles they were saying things like "Come on girl, not far to go now!" and "You're doing great!" etc. Linda had a "Hotpoint" T shirt on which brought her more than a few comments.

At about five miles we felt that we were gradually overtaking other runners, and this was a good feeling as we progressed through the multitude without apparently changing pace. I saw my husband at this point as well and that spurred me on. He wasn't expecting me so soon and hadn't got his camera in position which was a pity as that was to have been the only point where he could have captured me in full stride!

The drinks stations were a problem. I nearly always lost my companion and had to catch her up. She seemed to be able to get in and out very quickly, but I always seemed to have to queue. These points were a story in themselves, so I won't go into detail about my thoughts on 'drink stations.' The volunteers were doing a marvellous job in the circumstances.

Now to my knee. I started to get the first tinges of pain at about 5-7 miles, and I found if I ignored them, they would go away for a while but each time they came back they were more intense and finally at about 15 miles they began to give me real problems. I told Linda that I wouldn't be able to keep up with her any longer and our pace had now dropped so that we would be lucky to finish inside 4 1/2 hours, so she sped on ahead. I struggled on, keeping a watch out for any of my supporters, as I had missed my mother-in-law and sister-in-law at Tower Bridge, I just could not spot them in the crowds. I also found that it was getting cooler. It had been extremely hot even though we tried to get in the shade as much as possible. Finally at about 18 miles my knee was really painful, so I tried to tie my headband around it but that didn't work so I started to look for a first aid stop and slowed right down to a fast walk. I also saw my husband again at that point (camera at the ready) and he accompanied me to the first aid station where I was treated with ointment, a bandage and a few kind words. The few minutes rest must have helped a bit and I went back out on the road again. Once I actually got moving, I could run to the next drinks station without stopping but once I stopped for a drink, I found it ever so difficult to get started again. My running was more like hobbling by this time and I started thinking "So near but yet so far" and "I think I can. I think I can" just to keep pushing myself forward.

There by the side of the road, screaming and waving were my relatives, egging me on at 20 miles. I was getting there but I had now calculated that it would take about 4 3/4 hours, so whenever I had to stop jogging, I would walk by striding out as fast as I could. That didn't hurt my knee and perhaps I was able to walk faster than I could jog anyway. Many runners passed me, but I also passed many struggling on too. Some suffering from hitting the "Wall" and most seemed to have their knees bound up like me as well. Strangely many were to be left knees.

However, I was still enjoying myself just enjoying the day. Who would have thought I would have been here, the streets of London closed just for us to run on. The Mall came and that was the greatest moment of all besides the actual finish. Just to feel free to run towards Buckingham Palace which I was determined to do without stopping. The pain was numb by now and the greatest problem was to get started again after a stop. I walked around the corner into Birdcage Walk and started looking for the finish. I was gathering myself together for one final onslaught when a man came out of the crowd lining the Mall, took me by the shoulder and pointed to the finish. He said, "Look up the road girl, the finish is just up there, look at it and run straight to it." I remember smiling at him (you don't know what pain I'm in), but it worked, and I got back into some sort of stride and finally I was on the bridge. I could hear the loudspeaker saying, "you now have five minutes to cross the bridge if you want to finish in less than five hours." I just made it. It took me four hours and fifty-seven minutes and I placed around 14,000th.

My knee was badly bruised and made walking difficult for about two weeks afterwards but the rest of me felt fine. I suffered post marathon depression the next day but soon recovered and now I am wondering about the next one. I would very much like to experience the distance again without the problems of injury just to see if I could do four hours.

…………. END ………….

So, I went on with my running career. I ended up completing 13 marathons including the London Marathon five times, the Dublin Marathon and then the Seven Sisters and Beachy Head marathons which were all cross country. My best London Marathon time turned out to be 4 hours and 21 minutes, but I never managed to complete one in under 4 hours which had been my aim. The last full marathon I ran was in 2002 (aged 56) which was twenty years after my first one and also during those twenty years I completed many half marathons, the fastest being 1 hour and 49 minutes.

Figure 31: Running Guernsey Half Marathon

30- Working Life

New Hall Farm, Old Harlow

One of my tasks was to produce the farm statistics. I worked out the average prices of produce sold in the markets over a period of years, made comparisons between one market and another, one merchant and another, cost of transport, and so on. I kept the information on spreadsheets in big black binders and every week I would sit down with my grandfather and go over the figures with him. He would then decide if it was cost effective to keep growing a particular variety, increase or decrease the production of produce such as lettuce, runner beans, peas, sprouts or what acreage of potatoes to plant for the next year There were occasions when it was cheaper to plough a crop back in rather than spending time and money on wages and transport for no return. After several years and taking everything into account we finally accepted that the market gardening business was losing money. The net price of a simple box of cabbage had not increased for over fifteen years. We had the most efficient and latest equipment and fewer staff, but the costs of chemicals and fertilizers, packaging, transport and wages were ever increasing.

When our daughter, Ella was born, I would take her in her *Moses* basket and have her beside me in the office. At lunch time I would pop up to the house and have lunch with my grandfather. My step-grandmother had died by then, so it was company for him. I cherish all the memories of that house, even though I was often reminded of the steep and dangerous stairway which I tumbled down as a toddler.

Figure 32: Grandpa Soper 1896-1986

I was put in charge of keeping track of all the seeds, chemicals, fertilizers, and equipment which included tractors, lorries and vans. Every year we had to do a stock take and I had to chase up any anomalies and work out the depreciation for the accountants and auditors. It was an interesting job requiring a lot of concentration, burying my head deep into files and ledgers. I loved discovering things in the books. One time, I found that we had been receiving a small sum of money for a wayleave and I decided to find out what it was for. What a surprise when I found that it was for a telegraph pole in a field which was in Ely, Cambridgeshire. My grandfather had briefly rented some land there and a grading line for potatoes which had long since been sold, perhaps fifteen years before I came on the scene. The payments had been received and entered in a ledger, year after year, without anyone noticing. Mind you it was only about £1 per year so probably just got put into miscellaneous! I wrote to the Electricity Board so they would stop paying us and I guess we may have sent a refund.

It was a big task working on the valuations. Every detail about every single item on the farm, even to the amounts left in each container of insecticide, herbicide, oil, fertilizer, various bags and part bags of seeds, the vehicles and equipment and then the actual crops that were in the ground had to be recorded. Also, I had to make lists of the buildings on the date of the stock-take. Once the farm at Canes was bought and included there were around one thousand acres of crops and the two farms with buildings and equipment to register and value. It was time consuming even though I relied on the various members of staff to do the counting and I would then check the list against the previous year's stocks and any purchases made during the year. I then had to check the purchase price of each item and make the necessary adjustment as to value after depreciation. I have to say that even though it was a rather complicated task, I did enjoy working with the figures, balancing them and getting everything right.

The market garden business was subsequently ended, and we stopped growing vegetables, and converted the whole farm into grain but kept the rose growing. Wheat, barley and oilseed rape filled the fields at both New Hall Farm and Canes Farm. At the time we had also been growing rose bushes for more than twenty years.

We grew around 250,000 bare-root bushes and standards of about 30 varieties using contract workers from Holland who came to put the buds on the stocks and were known as 'budders.' The bushes were sold to several larger nurseries throughout the country and we even sent a yearly order to a nursery in Guernsey, Channel Islands.

My mother and I carried on with the rose business for several more years but there again, because the whole farm had been on rotation, following the seasons and supplemented by the market garden business, once one area was closed down, staffing became a problem. Finally, and sadly, we stopped growing roses as well. It was a wonderful time when the farm was busy. We had a farm office with a manager who had come to us having been in a similar role on a farm in Kenya. He had a secretary whose job I or my mother took over when she was away. Next door to his office was the accounts where I used an early version of a computer called a *Kienzler* to do the ledgers and also to process the wage slips from the time sheets. Next to that office was my grandfather's with his special leather chair, which I still have, and which was brought from London when his office at Spitalfields Market closed. We also had a small room for a telephone exchange with all the plug-ins, wires and ringers which I also operated when the telephonist was away. One of the jobs I must say I enjoyed was doing the analysis. I had the use of a very old-fashioned calculator, probably based on an original abacus which had a carriage I would click forward and a handle that I could turn either way for plus and minus. I learned to master the machine so I could quickly calculate percentages.

Figure 33: Mechanical pinwheel calculator

Later, of course, we moved on to electronic calculators and IBM computers as well as to a modern system for the telephones, both internal and external.

Another job I had over the years was to take the readings at a little weather station set up next to the farm offices. I would keep the records and then pass them on the to someone who kept all the records from around Harlow to process for the local weather forecasts and sent them to be included in the national statistics.

Going to meetings on behalf of the farm was a privilege for me. I attended annual Rose Growers Meetings at Harrogate, I went around with the inspectors to cover the farm, I attended a Peas and Beans conference at Chelmsford with the farm foreman and I even went to the Rose of the Year show in Surrey where I took part in voting for the name of the Rose of the Year. It was a lovely orange floribunda rose named Amber Queen. I was also honoured to be a judge for Mr. Tye's garden club at Sheering in their rose section. I was nervous about this because I didn't feel qualified, but he assured me that my choice was well received.

Another privilege for me was to accompany several of our long-term farm workers to the Essex Agricultural Show where they were given their long-term service awards to farming. One of them, Basil Field, had been working for my grandfather since before the war. He had gone off to serve his country and returned afterwards, preferring to continue working on the farm. I remember him arriving to work on his bicycle with a tattered great-coat held together with a binder-twine belt. He was a great character, but the war had made its mark on him. It was strange feeling for me to be called 'boss' when I could only think of the farm workers as colleagues just like my colleagues at work in Canada.

Once the office for the market gardening side of the business was changing there was less work for me, I was asked if I would go and work for West Essex Potatoes, a branch of West Essex Farmers, in their office in Epping, on a part time basis. It was 1974. They had been struggling with getting staff and at one of their meetings, my grandfather put me forward as someone who might be able to help on a part time basis. I still remained involved in the farm part time, often attending meetings with my mother and grandfather. I guess you might say that I was head-hunted as someone to put their office in order. It was a strange position to be in, but it did prove beneficial to the concern in the end.

I was mainly involved in checking their ledgers, invoices and other paperwork as well as attending their meetings with reports on my progress. The group had been formed by a number of Essex Farmers in order to coordinate the buying and selling of their potatoes. There were a couple of buyers who would go around the farms to view the potatoes that were being sold, checking the quality and grades before marketing them. They had a fleet of lorries which would then collect the potatoes and take them to the markets in London. I sometimes went to visit the farms too and got to know about the grading and whether the loads going up to the market matched the quality needed for the prices. I got great satisfaction from working there and found myself just one woman among dozens of Essex Farmers when there was a meeting. My first excursion into the unknown was when I accompanied my grandfather to a conference, and he suggested I made a little speech on his behalf or rather W. J. Soper Limited. Well, I did it and for me that was quite an achievement.

It wasn't long before I found there had been some incredible errors in the bookkeeping and several farmers had not been paid for their potatoes while others had been paid twice. When I first discovered it, I was quite shocked and went to the director. I had checked and double checked and found the errors went back several years. Unfortunately for one of the buyers he was found to be incompetent and was subsequently fired. I don't think there was any ill intention as he had not profited from it, but things had not been recorded and checked properly. One or two other staff members who were supposed to be checking and matching tonnages and payments lost their jobs as well and new staff had to be found. I was surprised that the auditors hadn't noticed the errors either.

I only worked there for about eighteen months because the company secretary for W. J. Soper Limited, Mr. Tye was retiring and I was offered his job. I therefore became the Company Secretary and I also became a director to my family's farming business.

When I first started working in the farm office, we were still using pounds, shillings and pence which were so much more difficult than the decimal currency I was used to in Canada. I soon became competent in using the 'old money,' but I am always reminded of how things changed in the few years I worked there. Everything seemed to be so antiquated to me, having experienced the computers and telephone systems in Canada. It was a bit like stepping back in time, however, during my time there everything was modernized to such an extent that the latest combine harvester purchased in 1983 had all the modern technology available to run it. Of course, there was a cost to match and a small house or apartment could have been bought for the price we paid. This may also have been the last straw when it came to the farm finances and the ability to make a profit. Shortly after we bought this monster of a machine, purchased more or less on the whim of the farm manager, we had to decide about how we carried on with the farm. He had managed to get us into the Essex Agricultural Society County Farm Competition for the best managed farm and we won second prize which was a great honour, but it came at a price. It was after this that we decided we would manage it ourselves, my mother and I, while everything was simplified with the idea to eventually place some if not the whole enterprise out to contract and no longer needed to keep employing him.

So, twelve years after I started working for the company, it was decided that the farm manager would have to move on. He was given notice and a generous severance package. I took on some of the role together with my mother. As a result, John and I moved from the house we had bought in Bishop's Stortford and settled ourselves into the farmhouse at Canes Farm where the farm manager had been living.

Here we made our home for the next 4 years and in 1984, Martin started his first job in London and on almost the same day our daughter Ella was born.

It was a large Georgian House with a central skylight and bay windows overlooking a pond. The house was divided in two

and the farm foreman, Derek Foster, lived in the spacious rooms at the back with his wife and we had the front with a large living room large dining room, kitchen with a lovely Aga, a walk-in pantry, basement store for apples and a kitchen garden.

Figure 34: Canes Farmhouse

It was a place to be. There was an old barn with lean-to which was a bit wonky due to the bomb damage as the farm was next to North Weald Aerodrome, a target during WW2. A large grain store had been built next to the pond with a drying facility for the grain which had a slatted hardwood floor. We always moved with the times and had to continuously invest in machinery and storage in order to compete by increasing production, growing the latest and best yielding crops but in the end keeping ahead, even with the subsidies, sales were dropping, competition increasing, we sometimes felt we were not getting anywhere with the investment.

My grandfather died in the summer of 1986, and it was decided that we would wind the farming down completely, sell off some of the land and put everything out to contract. The market garden business had been closed several years before and we had stopped growing the roses. During the winding down period from the market gardening to leasing out the farm we had to let a lot of staff go and that period of making redundancies was not a pleasant time. Both my mother and I both found it an exceedingly difficult period.

As Canes Farm was sold first, John and I had to move again and found ourselves back in Bishop's Stortford in a more modern house in Maple Close, quite a lot smaller than the farmhouse we had got used to. Ella started playschool close by in a building that still had 'Boys' and 'Girls' marked above its two entrances.

Figure 35: Maple Close, Bishop's Stortford

I was back to commuting to Harlow again and John went back to walking to work. By that time, the M11 motorway was in operation so the commute was a lot quicker, though perhaps not so picturesque. Canes farm was sold to a consortium of farmers. I kept going into the office to carry on with winding things up as there was still a lot to do at New Hall. The farmhouse was rented out and after a couple of years the unsold land was finally leased it to a neighbouring farmer.

I had become pregnant again and started staying at home more often so was able to go for lovely walks around Bishop's Stortford and meet up with friends. Martin had left home while we were still living at Canes Farm, at the time Ella was born. He had moved to London and went to work for a company at the London Stock Exchange. Inga was born in the summer and the birth went like a dream in comparison to when I had Martin, there being just over twenty years between them. Ella's birth had been a memorable one too, with the added fun of having had a team of student midwives observing the whole procedure, with my permission of course. They came to visit me the next day to see the baby and to thank me.

31- GUERNSEY

I had worked for the family farming business from 1971 until 1989 when we moved to Guernsey. I took up a new career of bringing up our two daughters, giving teaching assistance at their school, and for the last 19 years I've been a volunteer adviser and support worker for Guernsey Citizens' Advice.

Figure 36: Me with John at a nephew's wedding in 2017

I formed new friendships, joined the Guernsey athletic club, Guernsey Writers, and enjoy membership of the Guernsey Harriettes who run and socialize every week. I have travelled with the Harriettes to many events in the U.K., Europe and beyond.

I finally became a grandmother in June 2020 during the major world pandemic of 2020-2021.

Figure 37: Daughters - Ella and Inga - 2018

Figure 38: Mum at 80 with her 6 children

23 - A POEM

STONE
Beside my heart; the pump,
the one that circulates my blood,
there is another heart.

Not the heart guided by emotion,
but a gnarled, heavy, black, stone heart
invisible even to an X-ray.

It wasn't born with me,
just entered my body one day,
found its way through my skin

through an unguarded fissure,
reached the essence of me
before I could mouth my own name.

Beady as a cock-robin's eye at first,
this 'anti-matter' absorbing my childhood,
imploded to the size of the universe

until the 'real' heart; the pump,
the one that circulates my blood,
wanting to be rid of it, found a solution.

It started my body running
across fields, along riverbanks,
up gravel tracks, over the snows

into the medals on sports day
never good enough of course
always striving for the big burn.

The black-heart stone smouldered.
The body started marathoning
over the downs, into muddy ditches,

along highways, over cobbled streets
through green forests and desert dunes.
The black-stone heart caught alight

flamed up, burned down,
became smaller than a cock-robin's eye
and I opened my arms to my existence.

15/07/99

Jersey Arts, 2005 – Commended and published in their anthology.

MY WRITING AND PUBLICATIONS

As a child I expressed an interest in poetry and this is revealed by one of my teachers in one of my report cards. Unfortunately, I didn't keep any copies of the poems. I also told my grandfather in one of my special airmail letters to him that I wanted to be a poet when I grew up. However, I didn't start writing to any great extent until I had moved to Guernsey in 1989 aged 43 where I joined a local writing class.

Once I had started to produce some short stories and one or two poems, I discovered a Poetry Masterclass which was being held by the Cambridge Board of Continuing Education at Madingley Hall, near Cambridge. I sent off a sample of my poems and was accepted by the tutor, Roger Garfitt. Thus inspired, I continued to go to the classes once a year and for a few years even went twice. We studied different poets in great depth and then produced our own, hopefully inspired by them. We covered an eclectic mix of poets including Seamus Heaney, Louise MacNeice, Pablo Neruda, Marina Tsvetaeva, Tony Harrison, W.H. Auden, Ted Hughes and many, many more. I found the venue, which is a large country house with a kitchen garden and lovely grounds, to be a most peaceful place and a perfect setting for quiet contemplation and I was able to be quite productive, away from the pressures of a busy working life. I called it my yearly retreat and I hope to be able to attend another one before long.

I have now created almost a thousand poems. Now being 2020. They cover multitude of subjects and I have published many of them in magazines including Reach Publications, Ver Poets, Second Light Live, Artemis, The Poetry Society and locally in Guernsey. I have a collection of about 80 poems reflecting on my Canadian childhood experiences which I have called 'The River's Bend' but have yet to publish it. However, I did produce and have one collection published by The National Poetry Foundation in 2000 titled *'Wool-gathering'* ISBN 1 900726 610.

End Note: My father died alone of a stroke while living separated from his second wife in Norway. He never apologized or showed remorse for how he treated me.

Piero remarried, had a daughter Leanna, and died in Sarnia, Ontario, Canada having sadly gone blind and having lost a foot, both caused by his diabetes.

ACKNOWLEDGEMENTS

Roger Garfitt - Poet - My tutor at Madingley, Cambridge who has encouraged me in my poetry writing over many years at his ICE (Institute of Continued Education) Poetry Master Classes, Madingley, Cambridge.

Elizabeth Jean Knight née Soper - My mother – *Extracts from letters to her father.*

Gjennom villmark til krig (Wilderness to war) by Edvard Rennan – Published by Tiden Norsk Forlag ISBN 82-10-10857-4 (hf) – A translated version by Torolf Moen, edited by Diana Pritchard 2019 -not published.

Pippa McCathie – *Friend* who has published a series of her own books and kindly read through my early drafts and gave me tips and ideas.

Ron George – *Tsaskiy* - My childhood neighbour and friend for giving me information about the Wetsuwet'n clan in The Bulkley Valley. Author of *'The Fifth World'* – A story about his Wet'suwet'en family.

Keith Peters – *Brother of Erik Peters*, my first boyfriend. Keith informed me of what happened to Erik who died tragically in 1994. He also encouraged me to continue with my writings having read some of my poems.

Eileen Gaudion – Friend who has listened to my Canadian stories and shared interests over many years during our weekly walks.

POEMS

I would like to thank all my Canadian friends who welcomed me to the 'class of '64 reunion' in Smithers in August 2014 and made me finally feel accepted. Mary Jane Allen, Sheelagh Meiklem, Dianne Swift, John Rosberg, Larry Miller, John McDivitt, Roy Goheen, Jenny Elzinga, Margaret Horlings Tepstra, Joanne Heatherington, Bryan Dockrill, Dick Crowell and others keeping up our friendship including Vanda Monkman, Olza Then, LaVerne Egan, Mary Donaldson, Johanne Anderson, Margo Bates.

A special thank you to all my brothers and sisters and extended family for their support and understanding over the years, particularly my brother Jon who accompanied me to Cyprus during a most stressful time and my grandfather William James Fordham Soper for his generosity and trust in me.

Manufactured by Amazon.ca
Bolton, ON

25816322R00103